PORTABLE
CAREERS

PORTABLE CAREERS

Surviving Your Partner's Relocation

Linda R Greenbury

KOGAN
PAGE

First published in 1992

Kogan Page Limited
120 Pentonville Road
London N1 9JN

© Linda R Greenbury 1992

British Library Cataloguing in Publication Data

A CIP record for this book is available from the British Library.

ISBN 0-7494-0636-4

Typeset by DP Photosetting, Aylesbury, Bucks
Printed and bound in Great Britain

Contents

Author's Note   7

1. **Introduction**   9
   What is a portable career? 9; Who needs a portable
   career? 11; Relocation 12; Employment in a new
   location: the problems 13; Relocating partners: their
   needs 15; How to use this book 15

2. **Information About Yourself**   18
   Self-assessment exercises 19; Summary 29; Creating a
   career portfolio 29; Transferring skills from one area
   of life to another 32; Making action plans, setting
   manageable goals 37

3. **Searching For a Job in a New Location**   39
   Job search strategies 39; Starting the job search 40;
   Long-distance job searching 42; What you need to
   know about the new location 43; The advertised job
   market 46; The 'hidden' job market 47; Overview 50;
   Selected books and information resources for
   international relocation 50

4. **Employment on the Move**   57
   Flexible work opportunities 58; Professional specialists
   abroad 72; What else can a soldier do? 78; Resources
   for those retiring from paid work – early or on time
   82

5. Marketing Yourself   84
   Know your own resources 85; Presenting yourself
   attractively on paper 85; Adjusting your written
   presentations for portable careers 87; Interview skills
   for the highly mobile 96; Afterwards 99

6. Settling In   101
   The settling-in process 101; Developing a new
   personal support system 105; Maintaining home
   contacts 108; Settling in with work colleagues 109;
   Families 109; Dual-career couples 110; Singles 111

7. What Can You Do If You Cannot Work in Your
   Chosen Field?   113
   Overseas employment restrictions 113; When you
   cannot work 114; If you can work, but not in your
   chosen field 122; Self-employment and freelance work
   123; Telecommuting/teleworking 125; Flexible
   patterns of work 125

8. Further Aspects of Employment on the Move   127
   Is there any point in applying for a job now I am over
   50? 127; What to do about age on your CV 129;
   What can organisations do for working partners? 131;
   I've never heard of spouse assistance programmes –
   what are they? 133; Is career counselling worthwhile?
   134; What about me – a trailing husband? 138; How
   do I get a job when we go back home? 139

Afterword: Mobility and Equal Opportunities   141
   by Joanna Foster, Chair of the Equal Opportunities
   Commission

References   145

Useful Resources   147
   Books 147; Useful addresses 149; Career counselling
   services 153

Author's Note

This book has been inspired by many relatives, friends, colleagues and clients from Britain and America who helped me to understand how unconnected skills and interrupted plans eventually link together. For me, the answers came late in the day after many different schools and 'careers' – as a musician, children's fiction writer, mature student, bookkeeper, lecturer and career counsellor, as well as a long period as a traditional wife and mother.

My special thanks to June Bell, June Brown and James Greenbury for their unfailing support and encouragement. Also, to the British Diplomatic Spouses' Association for help with the 'Portable Careers' pilot project; the Institute of Careers Guidance for permission to adapt the Occupational Training Families poster; the Confederation of British Industries' Employee Relocation Council and Joanna Foster, Chair of the Equal Opportunities Commission, for permission to reproduce her speech from 'Relocation News' No 7; and Libra Studios, Twickenham, for artwork. Acknowledgement also to *The Guide for Occupational Exploration* and *The Occupational Outlook Handbook* 1990–91 edition, both compiled by The United States Department of Labor. To all of you and many others, thank you.

Finally, this book is dedicated to my late father, Harry, who had few choices in his life and to my best friends: my children Susan, James and Melissa whose options are so much greater.

Linda R Greenbury
April 1992

1. Introduction

What is a portable career?

A portable career is one that may be transferred from one location to another, with or without modification. It is flexible, adaptable and open-ended and it contains core or basic skills that may not be dependent on language, culture or local work conditions.

The notion of a portable career is not new. Several years ago, the Institute of Career Guidance issued a poster illustrating occupational training families (see Figure 1.1). Underneath the poster were these words: 'Training for a job family – rather than a single job – means you are better prepared for a changing world.' This caption is as meaningful today for portable work seekers as it was for yesterday's youngsters: acquiring a flexible range of skills makes one less dependent on a single job title. There were four main training families:

IDEAS: Scientific, Craft and Design and Food Preparation
PEOPLE: Personal Service, Community and Health
DATA: Administrative, Transport, Agriculture
OBJECTS: Installation, Processing, Manufacture.

As you work through this book, keep in mind these four categories and the eleven training families because they are helpful in assessing your own skills and making your portable career plans for the future.

Many others have added to the idea of transferable skills, including the best-selling American author, Richard Bolles. His

Figure 1.1 *Occupational training families*

annual publication *What Color Is Your Parachute?* has inspired job seekers and career professionals for over 20 years. The Project HAVE Skills programme, by Ruth B Ekstrom in the USA, conducted surveys with women and employers to create skills charts and tables relating Homemaking And Volunteer Experience (HAVE) skills to paid jobs. Other workers in this field of study, especially those concerned with career/life planning techniques – an overall appraisal of the total person with their work, family, leisure and home experiences – further contributes to portable careers.

At the core of a portable career is a person's understanding of what is meant by the word 'career'. In the early days of vocational guidance, choosing a career was a once-in-a-lifetime decision. Even now, many still think of a career as referring merely to their work life: their job title, their workplace, their paid employment. For them, and many others including a vast number of employers, unpaid work is not valid or 'proper' work. Later, researcher Donald Super and others, placed careers in the whole context of a human being's development and maturity until we came to realise that an individual's choice of a career unfolds over a period of time, sometimes continuing until mid-adulthood. And we recognise today how sensible it is to plan for several careers during a lifetime as a normal pattern of work experience. For the purpose of this book, the following definition is taken from Richard Bolles (1986): 'A job is a flexible combination of tasks whilst a career is a flexible combination of skills'.

Who needs a portable career?

Portable Careers is intended for several groups of people. First and foremost, this is a guide to employment for women who relocate because of a change in their partner's workplace. It is also for men in a similar situation when working women transfer to a new location. But, anyone – male or female – who finds their regular job disappearing for any reason whatsoever will also find useful material in the following pages. If you are about to retire, become redundant or resettled, or are thinking about a return to work after time away from the workplace, then you, too, may discover helpful suggestions to clarify your job-relevant strengths, identify effective skills and develop plans for the future.

The book is also relevant for employers and course leaders. International and domestic relocation personnel may offer it to employees and their partners, as may professional relocation services, expatriate resource centres, spouse assistance providers, workshops and seminars' co-ordinators. For those in charge of redeployment, when staff must seek opportunities elsewhere, *Portable Careers* contains a range of useful and positive ideas.

Relocation

Perhaps you are one of the increasing number of people moving jobs, homes and families. If so, you are not alone. The CBI Employee Relocation Council estimates about 250,000 people move home every year for work-related reasons, while many Britons – maybe up to 200,000 every year – go to work in another country. Some are relocated by their companies, within the UK or overseas, or move to take up new appointments; others face a group move, as organisations change premises. Some workers, particularly those without jobs, seek opportunities elsewere or accept relocation as an alternative to redundancy. And, as international boundaries alter and trade barriers fall, employees may have to work and live abroad.

In the past, employers usually relocated managerial and professional staff for career development and promotion reasons. Their wives, who became known as the 'trailing spouse', rarely worked outside the home and accepted a full-time support role to sole-breadwinner husbands. The 'trailing spouse' went where she was told and behaved in a predictable and dutiful manner.

More recently, a broader range of employees, specialist staff, management trainees and clerical workers as well as the high-flyers, are also being asked to move. Alongside the majority of these workers there are accompanying partners, male or female, married or in non-traditional relationships, who must also face the move. The 'trailing spouse' has now become the 'working spouse', with new priorities, a clear voice and a changed role.

There are more dual-earner couples in the labour market than ever before as over 50 per cent of UK households have incomes from both partners. At present, nearly half of the UK workforce are women with more expected as the supply of youngsters dwindles. Fewer than 10 per cent remain traditional stay-at-home wives with children, while the number of non-employed women without children is even smaller. Women work in virtually every profession and industry and at most employment levels. There are women MBAs, women high-flyers in banking and finance, women professionals (more than half new entrants to the Law Society are women), women in business (from the nationally famous Body Shop, to our friendly, local Mrs McMopps). Yes, there are many female part-timers, but they are not necessarily *unskilled* workers: a GP is still a highly qualified doctor even when working half-days only.

While it is true that the majority of relocated employees are usually accompanied by their wives, the traditional 'trailing spouse' is challenged once again when the partner who follows turns out to be a long-term co-habitee or a man. No longer is it enough for relocation personnel to worry about finding jobs for working wives. Women employees also transfer and their menfolk require portable careers, too.

Employment in a new location: the problems

If you are presently looking for work anywhere, in familiar or new surroundings, you should expect some special challenges. Competition from other job-seekers increases in times of economic downturn. You must adjust both professionally and personally to being without work. The loss of income is a major worry; friends and relatives may cause concern; the days and weeks often seem endless and you probably feel incomplete without a work role.

Job hunting in a new location is particularly complex. Unfamiliar with local recruitment strategies, you must rely on second-hand information to find a job, or take a chance by approaching friends of friends, contacting unknown firms directly, registering with strange employment agencies and even placing something about yourself in a 'Situations Wanted' column. Even within the UK there are variations in working practices, local culture, climate and customs. Working abroad incurs all these changes plus the adjustment to strange food, language, health, safety and social life.

The relocating employee often sees a transfer as a positive event, an exciting opportunity, a promotion, a challenge. For the accompanying partner, relocation is more likely to be a loss – loss of friends, family, neighbours, contacts, familiar surroundings, favourite recreations. As far as work is concerned, relocation means dislocation. You feel impotent, angry, frustrated and resentful as you lose control over your career and income. Perhaps it is impossible to secure another job at your current level in the same place as your partner and career continuity, promotion, business connections, a sense of identity and independence all seem to slip away from you. Even if you are not currently employed in a paid job but merely thinking about the possibility in future, you feel that relocation squanders all possible chances of continuing work.

The biggest problems appear to occur when a move is involuntary and imposed. Partners feel powerless and trapped and their options seem bleak: either you agree to move with an artificial smile while reluctance and resentment smoulder beneath the surface. Or, you put your foot down firmly and flatly refuse to be a part of the move. How, you ask, can you – as an accompanying partner – maintain workplace skills and career relevance when one or more transfers occur?

These are just some of the difficulties experienced by many individuals and their dependants who consider employment in new surroundings. Other reactions include stress, loneliness and depression; you will find some more about these in Chapter 6. Yes, there are disadvantages in relocation, but there are also opportunities and alternatives. This may be the chance of a lifetime to take a sabbatical, go back to school, try your hand at a hidden talent, enjoy the family, or offer your expertise on a volunteer basis. But this may not be a fulfilling life for everyone. Although many individuals work successfully anywhere they want, making the most of their potential and enjoying the challenge of a new location, they may not seem to have anything to do with your unique situation. All the same, it is worth bearing in mind that an open-minded, flexible attitude to mobility will improve your chances of making a success of any opportunities coming your way.

Portable Careers takes a closer look at employment on the move. By taking stock of your resources, you will find it easier to make an *informed* decision about your future, and create plans, goals and self-marketing strategies. *Portable Careers* is designed to offer you a third choice: make the move work positively for *you*.

Relocating partners: their needs

When a company plans to move its workforce to a new site, early preparation allows the organisation to arrange and promote the transfer in a positive way, giving employees and their families plenty of time to adjust to the change. But, quite frequently, an individual is required to fill a sudden gap in a far away office and must be relocated immediately. Then the working partner is assumed to be ready and able to drop everything, pack up and follow on.

Accompanying working spouses have two essential requirements before a transfer: information and contacts. Three types of information are required: first, information about the relocation decision, preferably at planning stage and before the decision is made to transfer. Second, information about the new location, that is everything about the physical, social and employment details, and, lastly, 'me' information: the assessment of individual transferable skills, careers goals, life plans. Contacts are necessary for all job-seekers whether or not they are moving to a new location; for transferring spouses they are vital lifelines, enabling individuals to keep in touch with home and create new links in the host environment.

Portable Careers contains practical advice about all these aspects of information and contacts to help partners respond to the move, adapt to the new location and have a more meaningful portable life.

How to use this book

The background of this book is based on individual career planning programmes, workshop courses and pilot projects with accompanying spouses in high mobility situations, such as partners of military personnel (who move about every couple of years), the foreign service, corporate settings and government departments.

The following chapters contain self-help exercises, an ideas bank, self-marketing strategies and a resources guide. Commence with Chapter 2: Information About Yourself. This self-assessment section is an essential starting point for the creation of portable careers. It will help you to take stock of your resources and give you better information upon which to take decisions about your future. Once you have worked through all the exercises, turn to the summary page and complete it. Then read on about transferring your skills. Do not forget the occupational training families mentioned earlier in this chapter as you create action plans and set goals for the future.

Chapter 3 looks at Searching For a Job in a New Location. Here you will find tips and information about distance work opportunities, both within the UK and abroad. In Chapter 4, there are four sections: details of work that travels well, a summary of professional specialists abroad, ideas for transferring military experience to civilian careers and some suggestions for retirees.

Chapter 5 is a comprehensive self-marketing section, pointing you in the direction of appropriate job application styles for Britain, the USA and Australia, together with advice about covering and thank-you letters and interview skills. Chapter 6, Settling In, explores ways of developing a new social circle and support system, and of fitting in with new work colleagues.

Chapter 7 is for those who cannot work in their chosen field and has suggestions for maintaining career continuity through non-paid work, education and training. Here you will also find information about self-employment and flexible patterns of work. Chapter 8, the final one, covers various special relocation issues including spouse assistance from organisations, what to do about awkward questions in job applications, finding a career adviser, the trailing husband and singles abroad. A list of useful resources follows on page 147. It provides addresses for the organisations mentioned in the book and publication information for books.

However, *Portable Careers* is not a book with magic answers or comprehensive solutions to every individual predicament. Some readers may need personalised one-to-one vocational guidance. Work through the exercises first and take them with you to show your adviser before taking further tests. At the end of the day, the hard truth may be that your particular career will not travel. Then, your professional helper should be able to suggest a range of retraining suggestions to complement and enhance your existing experience and knowledge. Counsellors may also offer personal and emotional support during the period of change. If you wish to obtain professional help in finding your portable career, turn to Chapter 8 for career counselling guidelines.

A final word: *Portable Careers* illustrates how to identify your transferable capabilities and suggests how they may be applied from one area of life to another. It is not an overall career assessment book. There are several excellent career/life planning workbooks widely available for personal stock-taking, retirement, career change and so on. If you feel you require a career/life planning workbook, look in the public library careers section or approach a quality book shop for recent publications, including those listed on page 147.

2. Information About Yourself

Someone once described trying to launch a career without first taking stock of one's skills and resources as being similar to driving a car without a steering wheel!

Every individual is unique, with their own array of talents, assets, qualities and traits. There are inborn, natural abilities and special knacks which come easily to some but are often unacknowledged and taken for granted: the 'natural' cook, 'talented' musician, 'born' public speaker. Then there are broad areas of work-content skills: our technical abilities, formal training and specialised aptitudes. When we talk about a skilled worker, we usually mean work-content or employment-specific skills. And there is yet another, third range of skills: our functional or interchangeable capabilities. These are many of our portable skills, the skills that travel best and the ones we shall focus our attention on most closely here. You will find more details of this type of skill later in this chapter.

Taking stock of your skills and resources requires personal time. For the best results, overview this chapter quickly in order to gain a 'flavour' of the exercises, then allow yourself a period of time when you will not be rushed or interrupted, have plenty of working space, and feel relaxed and comfortable. Have ready plenty of paper, pens, pencils, some highlighters or coloured crayons as well as a folder in which to store your work. Undertake each exercise slowly: few of us remember all about our past at one go so let yourself wander down memory lane and reflect back on your life whenever necessary. Do not worry about making mistakes or adding additional details later. The more information you are able to include, the better equipped you will be to take advantage of the ideas expressed in this book.

There are *no* 'good' or 'bad', 'right' or 'wrong' answers to any of the following exercises. For the moment, it is irrelevant where you acquired your skills. It does not matter if you learned at home, at college, in the workplace, as a child or as an adult or what was anyone else's opinion of your prowess, or lack of it. Focus now on jogging your memory and placing on paper as much detail and data about yourself as possible.

You may be wondering about sharing the exercises with a partner or friend. Another person's view is often most helpful, as they see you in a different light from the way you see yourself. All the same, please do not ask anyone else to help unless you feel sure you can cope with some surprise replies or if it is going to start a family rumpus! Your answers are private to you unless and until you wish to share them. The only person you need to be completely honest with is *yourself*.

Self-assessment exercises

The flow chart of your life

The first step in the self-assessment process is to survey your work/life experience by creating a personal panorama of your life. The flow chart of your life is a mini-biography in note form, highlighting important events and clarifying significant experiences.

1. Using a large piece of paper, draw a series of boxes connected by arrows, as illustrated in Figure 2:1.

2. Start with the box at the top, left-hand side. Inside this box, place the place and date of your birth together with any details about your birth which you feel are important.

3. In the next box, write about your childhood and education. If you moved home or school or had any other major change in your life, use a new box.

4. Continue in this way, adding a fresh box for every new life

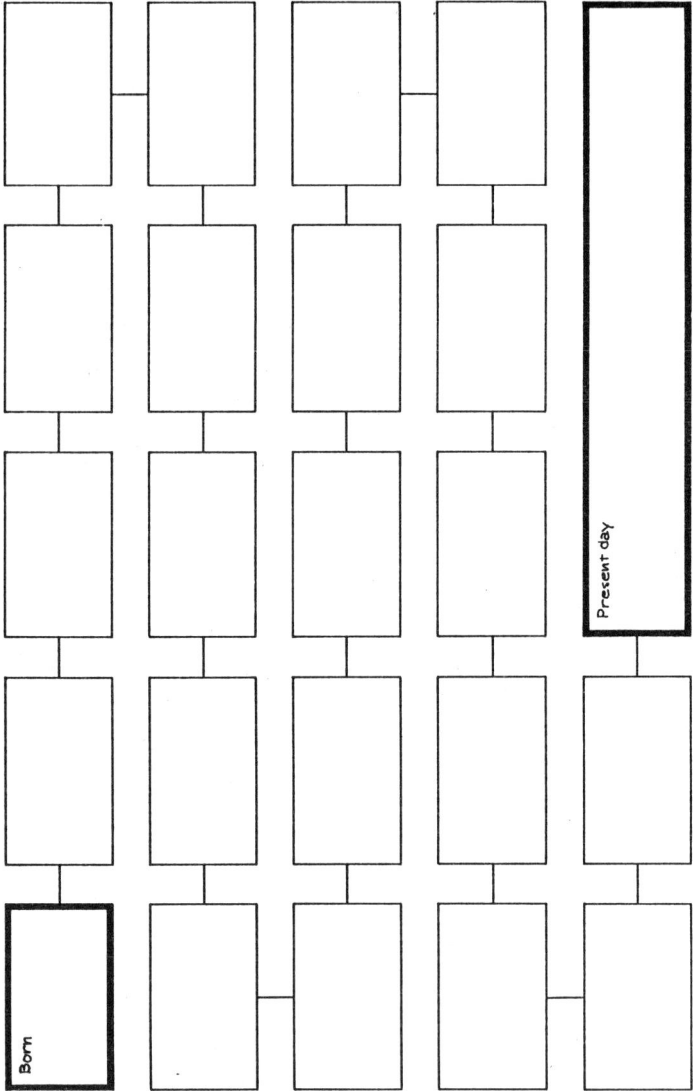

Figure 2.1 *Empty flow chart*

stage, until you reach the present day – your current situation. Note any qualifications, achievements, commendations, prizes, awards, relocations, jobs, family changes and so on. Include any special happenings – nice or nasty. Gradually flesh out the skeleton of the flow chart until it satisfactorily represents your life/work experience. You can add boxes and arrows or change their direction if you wish. Use as much paper as necessary.

5. When the flow chart of your life is complete up to and including the present day, stand back and evaluate it. Use highlighters to note

- pleasant experiences
- less enjoyable experiences

6. Look now at your highlighted experiences, both the pleasant ones and the less enjoyable. Think about the personal qualities which you used to cope with and manage these events and write them on a separate sheet. The following list is intended to help identify a few personal qualities; add more of your own.

Activity-orientated	Adventurous	Caring
Clever	Compassionate	Conscientious
Co-operative	Creative	Decisive
Down-to-earth	Efficient	Enterprising
Enthusiastic	Factual	Fair
Friendly	Idealistic	Independent
Loyal	Outspoken	Patient
Pleasant	Practical	Quick
Realistic	Reliable	Responsible
Restless	Sensitive	Spontaneous
Supportive	Tough	Traditional

7. Later in the self-assessment process, you will extend your flow chart into the future. Using a similar box-and-arrow style, think about how you would like life and work to continue if you:

- could just please yourself
- take into consideration partners, children, close relatives
- take into consideration education, training, qualifications

Table 2.1 *Satisfactions table*

Satisfaction	Work	Home/Family	Leisure
Achievement			
Adventure			
Affection			
Approval			
Challenge			
Companionship			
Competence			
Competition			
Excitement			
Flexibility			
Generosity			
Glamour			
Helping society			
Honesty			
Humour			
Identity			
Independence			
Leadership			
Money			
Popularity			
Power			
Recognition			
Responsibility			
Risk taking			
Security			
Spirituality			
Stability			
Team work			
Tranquility			
Variety			

- take into consideration employment downturns or developments
- continue with your present lifestyle

Satisfactions

We often speak about 'job satisfaction' but it means many different things to different people. For most of us, paid work is a necessary way of paying the bills and using our qualifications and training, but while one person gains great enjoyment from a large salary cheque, another prefers to help others regardless of salary. What will give *you* job satisfaction – in both work and non-work situations? The following exercise will help you begin to clarify your needs and your expectations from work, relationships and play.

1. Table 2.1 lists a number of 'needs' which many people feel they would like fulfilled and the three major areas of life: work, home/family and leisure. Think about how you feel about each need and in which area of your life that need could be achieved. (*Note*. The table is necessarily incomplete as satisfactions are unique to each individual. Add any other items as necessary.) Rate each need on the following scale:

    3 of no importance for this area of my life
    2 of some importance for this area of my life
    1 of great importance for this area of my life

2. Once you have completed the table, highlight your six most important needs for each life area.

3. Compare your three lists. Are many of the items similar, or do you require different satisfactions from each life area?

4. Ask yourself: To what extent have you gained satisfaction from your past employment, home/family and leisure pursuits?

5. To what extent does your present situation fulfil your needs?

6. To what extent will your new location meet your needs?

7. How many of your most important needs or satisfactions may be transferred to a different life area – after relocation, for example?

Skills

'I haven't any training, I can't work.'
'I've always been a nurse/mechanic/salesperson, so I can't do anything else.'
'I'm only a secretary – no other qualifications. . . .'
'I can't do anything really well.'

Do these remarks sound familiar to you? People from many different occupations and at many different levels of employment – from burned-out professionals to stagnant secretaries – have muttered these phrases, as have those who seek work without success. They share a common problem: they think of employment in terms of only *one* kind of skill – *work-content* skills.

Work-content skills are only part of the story; we need to dig deeper into ourselves to discover the vast reservoir of 'experiential learning', our unsung and diploma-less abilities which we have acquired from other areas of life – apart from the workplace. Understanding more about your skills will increase your marketability.

Everyone has strengths as well as limitations since people learn a great deal from everyday living as well as from their actual jobs. Many people, particularly women, undervalue themselves, after absorbing a stream of negative or de-motivating messages from early in life. Later on, lack of career education may suggest that no rewarding work is available without qualifications, just dead-end or unskilled jobs.

The exercises below will assist you in identifying skills from many areas of your life – paid work as well as home, family and community activities. Do not limit yourself by thinking only about employment skills or abilities for which you have qualifications.

The role tree
The role tree exercise is not, as some may imagine, an exercise in artistic expression! Instead, it is a creative method of helping you to find out your hidden talents and skills. Use a large piece of paper to draw the role tree framework or copy the outline from Figure 2.2.

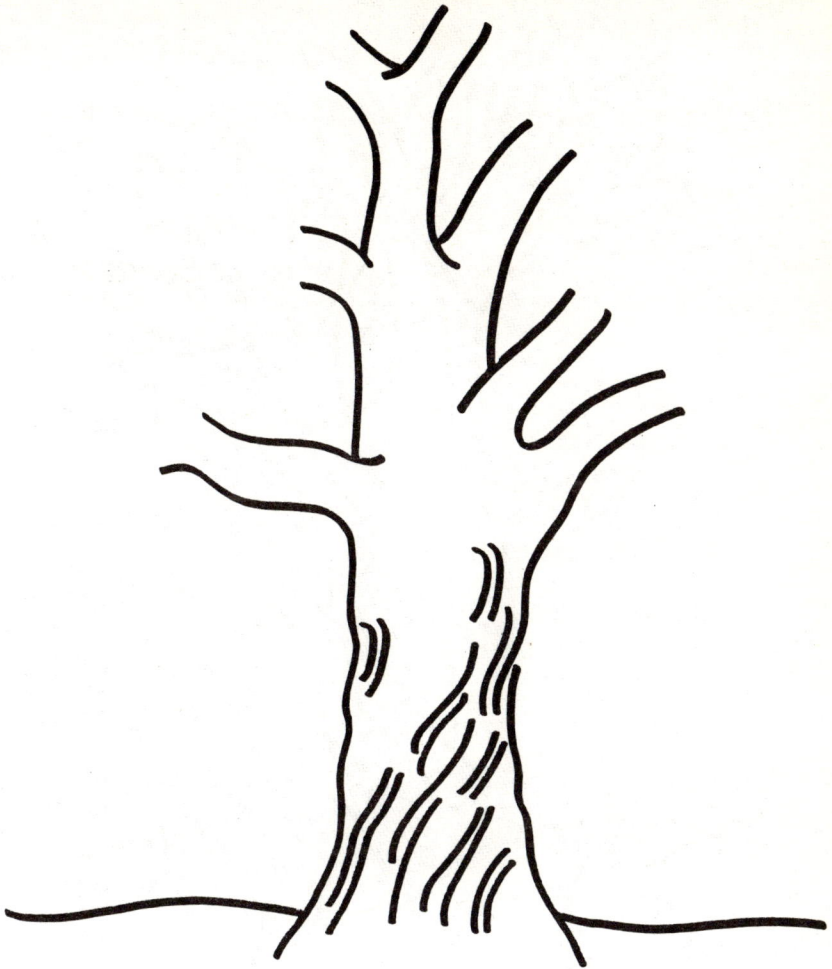

Figure 2.2 *Role tree framework*

1. Draw the branches of the tree. Each branch represents one role which you play (or have played) in your life, eg: a childhood 'branch', parent, spouse, friend, worker, sports person and so on.

Most people have seven or more roles. Do not rush this part of the exercise; include your past roles as well as present day ones. Allow your memory to wander, ask others, take your time and include *all* your various roles. These branches represent who you *were* or *are* now.

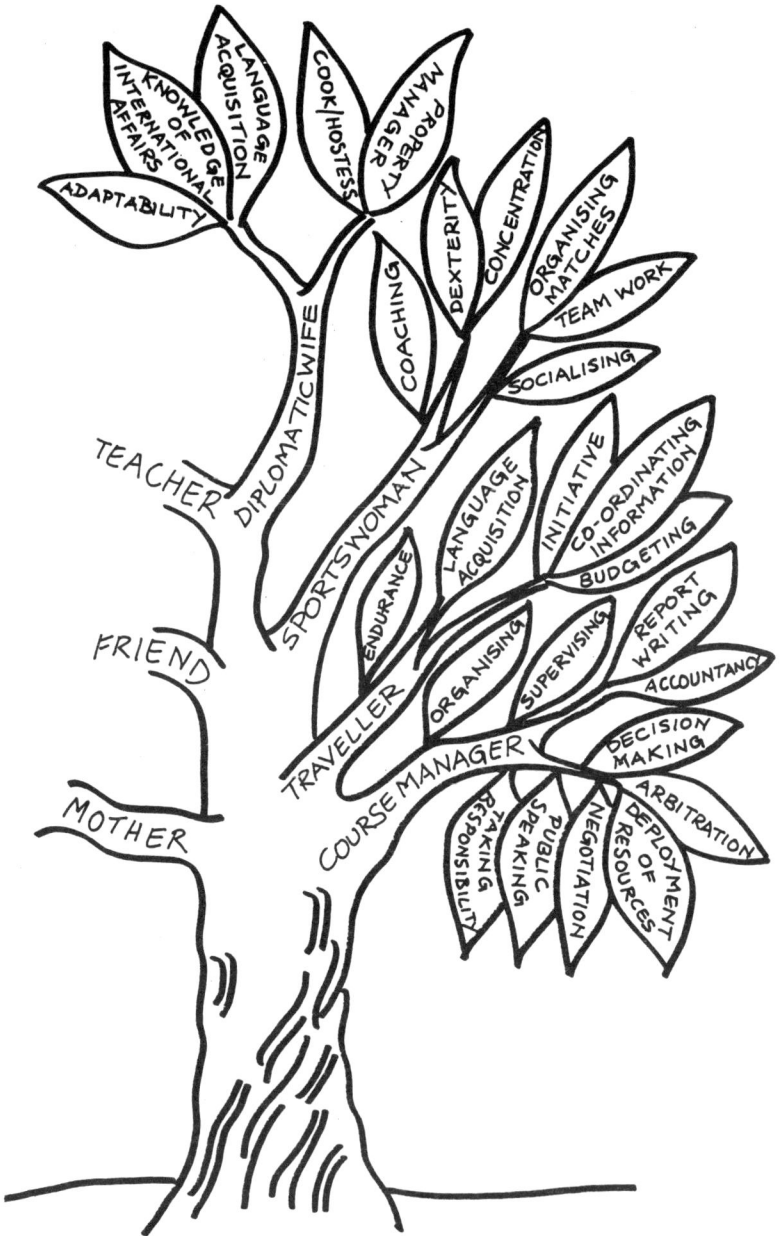

Figure 2.3 *Half-completed role tree*

2. For each branch draw in some smaller branches and 'leaves' (you can use cartoon bubbles or diagrams if you prefer). What did/do you do when you were/are involved in that role? The leaves represent what you *do* or *have done* (see Figure 2.3). Write a skill verb in each leaf to describe your action or activity. Try to be as specific as possible.

Here is a selection of skill terms to help you with the role tree; there are many more:

Advising, analysing, assembling, assessing, budgeting, classifying, communicating, compiling, constructing, co-ordinating, deciding, demonstrating, dexterity, evaluating, influencing, initiating, innovating, instructing, leading, motivating, negotiating, organising, persuading, planning, prioritising, recruiting, remembering, repairing, researching, selling, strategic thinking, stress management, supervising, systematising, teamwork, tending.

3. On a separate piece of paper, list your skill verbs. Grade your competence in each skill by underlining in different colours. Pay particular attention to those skills that occur most often.

4. Finally, on a fresh sheet, make a new list of all your skills under the following headings:

Your *favourite* skills – the ones you *enjoy* using
Your *high grade* skills – the ones which you can do *well*
Your *moderate grade* skills – the ones you can do *fairly well*
Your *low grade* skills – the ones you are *least able* to perform or dislike
. . . and – very important – Skills you wish you could do *better*.

Work skills
Employers usually require a full work history when you send in a job application. Traditionally, they expect to see details about each of your past employers, your previous work titles and your job responsibilities.

For the purpose of this self-assessment review (and for later job-search and self-marketing use) you should know as much as possible about your achievements in the workplace. This exercise reviews your *paid* work experience, but concentrates not only on

Table 2.2 *Skills acquired from paid work: job no:*

YOUR JOB TITLE

ORGANISATION SIZE

PUBLIC/PRIVATE SECTOR?

TASKS INVOLVED

TRAINING ATTENDED

NEW SKILLS LEARNED

OLD SKILLS IMPROVED

KNOWLEDGE GAINED

SOCIAL SKILLS ACQUIRED

GOOD THINGS ABOUT
THE JOB

WHAT DID *YOU* CONTRIBUTE
TO THE FIRM?

ADD HERE ANYTHING ELSE
IMPORTANT ABOUT THIS JOB

your job descriptions but on your learning activities and contributions as well.

For each *paid* job, assess the skills you acquired, using the format illustrated in Table 2.2. Use a new page when necessary.

Interests, hobbies and leisure skills
The questionnaire in Table 2.3 looks at your skills acquired from spare time pursuits. You may have learned some of your interests at courses, workshops or other places where you received tuition from an experienced teacher. Alternatively, you may have read 'How To Do It' books to learn other hobbies; perhaps friends showed you how – to play card games, for example; or maybe you are self-taught. Complete the questionnaire by ticking in the appropriate columns as indicated. Add additional interests or hobbies as necessary. Review your completed questionnaire: How many ticks under each column? What does this indicate about your preferred learning style?

Summary

The summary matrix (Table 2.4) will help you assemble all your self-assessment material. Use your answers to the previous exercises to fill in every section.

Creating a career portfolio

During your self-assessment exercises, you will have referred back to various documents. It is sensible to make several photocopies of these credentials and assemble them, together with the originals, in a large folder. You should include:

Your self-assessment material
References from past employers
Recommendations from customers, tutors, clients, superiors
Past and present CVs
Copies of cover and thank-you letters
Copies of job application blanks and completed forms
Press reports on any of your activities
Details of any publications under your name
Awards and certificates

Table 2.3 *Interests, hobbies and leisure skills questionnaire*

Interest/Hobby	Self-taught	From books	From friends	Took a course	Other (How?)
Acting					
Bookkeeping					
Car maintenance					
Carpentry					
Crochet					
Darts					
Debating					
Design buildings					
Design clothes					
Design machinery					
Develop photographs					
Drawing					
Dressmaking					
Drive – HGV					
Drive – motor car					
Drive – other vehicle					
Electrical work					
Enjoy crosswords					
Football					
Gambling					
Gardening					
Give first aid					
Graphic design					
Household repairs					
Invent gadgets					
Knitting					
Listening to problems					

Table 2.3 *continued*

Interest/Hobby	Self-taught	From books	From friends	Took a course	Other (How?)
Mountain climbing					
Needlework					
Oil painting					
Organise Brownies/ Cubs					
Paint a room					
Pet care					
Play musical instrument					
Play bridge					
Play chess					
Plumbing					
Print photographs					
Public speaking					
Raise funds					
Ramble					
Religious activities					
Repair machinery					
Research family history					
Ride a bicycle					
Ride a horse					
Sail					
Shorthand					
Sing solo/in choir					
Snooker					
Swimming					
Tailoring					
Tennis					
Typing·					

Table 2.3 *continued*

Interest/Hobby	Self-taught	From books	From friends	Took a course	Other (How?)
Water-colours					
Wine making					
Write features					
Write drama					
Write fiction					
Write poetry					
Yoga					
TOTAL TICKS:					

Academic qualifications and transcripts
Workshop and course details
Samples/photographs/exhibition catalogues of your work

As you continue work – paid or unpaid – add the detailed records of each employment to your career portfolio. Always keep it up to date. Take your career portfolio with you on your travels but retain an additional copy in a safe place in case of emergencies. If you are relocating overseas and are married, you should also include copies of your birth and marriage certificates. A number of passport sized photographs is also useful.

Transferring skills from one area of life to another

Note the case of the retired Army Officer who, after successful World War Two campaigns, returned home to regiment his

Table 2.4 *Summary page*

The flow chart of your life
Write here your six most transferable personal qualities:

1 ....   2 ....

3 ....   4 ....

5 ....   6 ....

Satisfactions
List your six most important needs for each life area:

	Work	Home/Family	Leisure

1 ....

2 ....

3 ....

4 ....

5 ....

6 ....

The role tree
Your *favourite* skills:

Your *high grade* skills:

Skills you wish you could do *better*:

Work-content skills
Your *favourite* work-content skills:

Your *high grade* work-content skills:

Table 2.4 *continued*

Work-content skills you wish you could do *better*

Interests/hobbies/leisure activities
Your *favourite* hobbies:

Your *high grade* interests:

Leisure activities you wish you could do *better*:

Finally write here any further comments, accomplishments, talents, competences and qualities which you have not already mentioned.

family. Military-style, NCO wife had to 'jump to it' (what, exactly, was never precisely explained) and the lower children-ranks received orders, to be obeyed – at the double. Such rule-by-dictat seems an undesirable lifestyle, yet there is one thing to recommend it: it is an excellent example of how to transfer skills from one area of life to another.

To transfer your skills from one area of life to another requires two stages: first, creating a list of your own resources and, second, understanding the kind of jobs and careers that use your skills. The exercises earlier in this chapter were intended to help you to take stock of your resources; the second stages will be discussed later in this chapter. Now, look at your skills in more detail:

The occupational training families poster in Chapter 1 (Figure 1.1) showed 11 job families, grouped under four major headings:

- Ideas
- People

- Data
- Objects

Here is a small selection of skills (there are lots and lots more) from each category:

- *Skills primarily with Ideas:* Improvising, adapting, designing, intuition, creating, innovating.
- *Skills primarily with People:* Taking instructions, serving, sensing, communicating, persuading, performing.
- *Skills primarily with Data:* Observing, evaluating, analysing, organising, classifying, researching, calculating.
- *Skills primarily with Objects:* Fixing, repairing, driving, being athletic, working with the earth and nature, using (tools).

Review your skills collated on the summary page (Table 2.4) and initial *all* your skills with an I, P, D or O. How many do you have in each category? Look at your favourite skills: do they form part of a job family? Similarly, compare the list of skills you wish you could do better to the training families. Check which job families combine and consider if your existing talents will expand to take up a larger slice of the diagram. If, for example, you possess many Ideas skills, these could be used in manufacturing, science, craft and design, food preparation and even some areas of personal service.

The second step in transferring skills to a new life area is to find descriptions of typical jobs and careers. I am frequently surprised to discover how little individuals appear to know about ways of researching jobs and careers. The following represents a succinct version of my favourite lesson on the topic!

- Ask people in jobs which interest you
- Consult your local Careers Office and ask for access to
  - Factsheets on various jobs
  - Their information resources
  - 'Signposts' card index
  - Videos, microfiche and computerised material
- Consult your local adult education college
- Go to the reference library and browse through the careers section

- Read books such as:
  - *An A – Z of Careers and Jobs* (although intended for school and college leavers, this is a useful starting point describing more than 350 jobs and each entry gives details of personal qualities needed)
  - *The Penguin Careers Guide* (comprehensive information for youngsters, adult career change and re-entry)
  - *Occupations*: an annual publication published by COIC, available direct or from Careers Offices

A portable career also requires job-relevant skills. *Job-relevant* skills include the following:

- Organisational, managerial and leadership skills
- Technical and professional skills
- Recreational and cultural skills
- Health, education, welfare, elderly, counselling type skills

Many people are confused about whether skills acquired in the home can be used in the workplace. While it is certainly true that many domestic competencies are indeed management skills, and the only differences between them are the context or place where they have been acquired and the language in which they are described, the business community finds it difficult to take these accomplishments seriously.

It is always depressing for anyone to be rejected for a job, especially so when you have tried your hardest to find work over a long period. What can be done to help those with unusual or non-traditional experience? Employers need to reconsider their recruitment criteria by accepting non-paid work in the same way as regular salaried employment. They could produce more flexible job application forms, with more importance placed on applicants' skills and less prominence on dates and ages. At the same time, job-seekers must help themselves. They improve their chances of gaining work when they learn how to market themselves, using the language employers recognise and offering commercially credible experience to validate their skills.

Therefore, if your skills repertoire has gaps or you lack sufficient convincing experience to apply for a job now, look for a short-term paid opening which offers scope either to acquire the missing skill(s) or a chance to enhance your credibility – or both. Education and/or training is another alternative route: it will create a bridge between old, rusty or missing skills and new ones. Course tutors and fellow students also provide valuable contacts and networking opportunities. Volunteer posts, part-time, temporary or short contract assignments are similarly useful.

The most significant point to remember is this: whatever route you decide upon must enable you to obtain practice, references and experience in the required skill(s) in order for future employers to take your application seriously.

Making action plans, setting manageable goals

We often set ourselves goals and draw up action plans without realising it. A participant in the Portable Careers pilot project described her preparations for the family Christmas thus: 'I am a "list person". I use them to help me plan what I am going to do, to clear my mind on certain problems, as a checklist and reminder system and they also make it easier for everyone else to know what is happening at a given time. At the same time I do not regard them as the last word and am very good at adapting things or changing them at the last moment if necessary.' She went on to describe her menu list and freezing/cooking timetable in great detail, starting in October (cakes, pies and puddings made), November (buying and freezing food, checking and replenishing stocks) to December (order and shop for fresh food, bakery, meat, dairy products). She included her kitchen action list for the few days before Christmas which she pins up in the kitchen for everyone to read: 'All hands to help with washing up!'

How do you prepare for Christmas? Are you as well organised as the example above, or do you just muddle through? Christmas, of course, is just one specific goal and the ideas above are good examples of action planning. When goals and action plans, those lists and timetables, are put together, they create a sense of direction, set out clearly defined objectives and give a sense of order in what may well be a time of chaos and upheaval.

Action plans and goals can be made about anything, although

it is easier to categorise them into groupings. You could have 'career' goals and plans, 'personal development', 'family' or 'education and retraining' – whatever you find is appropriate in your life at the time. Planning periods are usually short term (1 month, 6 months), medium term (1 year, 3 years) or long term (5 years, 10 years, 20 years).

If you want to try your hand at action planning, write down exactly how you prepare for the family Christmas or going on holiday or any similar happening for which you make special arrangements. You may be surprised to find how much time you spend planning – in your mind, if not on paper – to be ready for the great day.

Specific goals are very useful for portable careers. To create manageable goals and action plans for portable careers, begin by choosing a short-term goal, one that you will achieve with reasonable confidence and success. Aim, for example, to find out more about a specific job. Plan your actions in small steps:

- go to the library
- speak to the librarian
- ask for relevant books
- read the books
- take notes and/or photocopies
- follow up leads for more information
  and so on.

Tell other people what you intend to do and get their support. Stay flexible to allow yourself to adjust to difficult or unexpected circumstances. Give yourself credit when the goal is reached – and then set another one straight away!

3. Searching For a Job in a New Location

Job search strategies

Job search strategies are not always included in career education programmes, so you may be unfamiliar with some of the more effective methods to use. The best known method, but possibly the least useful, is to read the Situations Vacant advertisements in the newspapers and journals and answer those which seem to fit your qualifications, age, experience and so on. This involves numerous letters, CVs, telephone calls, application forms and, all too often, disappointments. You wonder what else you can do. You hear mutterings about the 'hidden job market', but do not know where or what it is. Who can help? What questions should you ask? How do you start?

While there is no one method to guarantee a successful job-hunt, many of the following ideas are intended to broaden your options and assist your employment potential.

The Golden Rule for finding a job in a new location is:

START THE JOB SEARCH BEFORE YOU LEAVE HOME

First of all, do your homework about yourself. Clarify the skills and competencies that *you* are able to offer an employer. Unless you are absolutely clear about your own strengths and motivations, you are unlikely to present a convincing image to an employer. If you have any doubts about your resources, go back to the self-assessment exercises in the previous chapter. Should you remain unclear after completing Chapter 2, obtain professional help.

Starting the job search

Start the job search as near to home as possible. Look first to your present or recent employer. How much help is available there?

Relocation

As an accompanying partner, you are one of the key people involved in relocation who may make or break settling-in time, job performance, corporate image and the company's financial investment. The organisation should want to convince you the relocation will succeed but it cannot do so if you are invisible or silent. Ask about the relocation at the earliest opportunity. If the transfer decision has yet to be finalised, determine who is discussing what with whom, when matters are likely to be decided and whom you can talk to about it. Find out who will be managing the relocation (company staff, consultants, other agents?) and details of any proposed meetings, seminars, briefings, on-site visits, videos, exhibitions.

Enquire about spouse assistance programmes: what is available for you, how do you obtain it, who pays? (There is more detail on spousal assistance in Chapter 8, page 133.) If you have heard only recently about the relocation, it may be because the employer has been hesitant to intrude into personal and family matters or it could be that letters were sent to you but have been mislaid, lost or forgotten. Do not assume the company does not care about you before checking with your partner for company letters or circulars. Take matters into your own hands and discover if you have been missing out on anything important.

If you are invited to the office for a chat, with or without children, you may wonder whether or not to accept. Could your concerns jeopardise your partner in some way or appear unprofessional? Always welcome an opportunity to meet on a friendly basis, but prepare the ground sensibly. Leave the youngsters behind and suggest an alternative meeting in an informal setting at a time and place agreeable – and relaxing – to you. Write down a list of questions to ask and prepare to answer questions yourself; it is not necessary to commit yourself to relocation at this stage so leave your options open. Open-ended questions that invite an explanation or description (How? What? When? Where?) are less confrontational than closed questions – those requiring just a simple 'yes' or 'no' answer. Discuss the organisation's communication (or lack of it) with spouses via letters, invitations, support groups, in-house magazine articles and features. Find out who you should approach in the future – a contact name and number – should you require more information.

Military resettlement

You are strongly advised to obtain all possible help and assistance *before* you leave the armed forces; after you have 'gone through the door', that is, left the Service, the Ministry of Defence is no longer responsible for you. The biggest defence cuts are expected in the Army, with smaller numbers from the Royal Air Force and Royal Navy and most will be from the United Kingdom. Some redundancies will be compulsory, phased over several years; others will occur by 'wastage'. However, all expect to have advance notice of the change, but note that those who apply voluntarily are less likely to have a long period between giving notice and discharge.

Find out who is in charge of resettlement and ask about resettlement briefings, action support centres and road shows on careers, housing, finance and civilian life. Enquire when attachments to civilian firms and courses will take place; if any non-military consultants are available; who will be your outplacement adviser; if counselling is available, and about links with the Royal British Legion, and the Soldiers', Sailors' and Airmen's Families Association (SSAFA).

If you are a military spouse, you are quite likely to find yourself the mainstay of the family during – and after – the resettlement period. You could even become the family breadwinner while your partner retrains. Both of you should ask for and obtain as much information as possible. Questions should include employment, education and training opportunities in the area in which you live now, as well as in future locations. Overseas wives should keep in contact with home-based Wives Federations/Groups, read the journals and newsletters, and look out for new initiatives regarding retraining grants and opportunities.

Long-distance job searching

Searching for a job across countries and continents means many letters, telephone calls and, possibly, travelling to meet employers face-to-face.

Writing

You do not have to write hundreds of letters and run up a huge postage bill to find a job far away from home. There are ways of making the process more manageable. To start with, obtain plenty of information about firms in the new location. Go to your nearest central reference library and look for directories (see sources of information section below), publications, addresses of local agencies and Chambers of Commerce and other background material for the new location. Then write brief, polite target letters to individuals (obtain these from company literature) requesting general information (annual report, company newsletter). Do not include your CV or life history at this stage. Make sure the letter is typed or hand-written legibly, check for accuracy, include your name and address (with postcode) and enclose a stamped addressed envelope or International Reply Coupon as a courtesy. Should you receive an encouraging response, then is the time to write back with a CV or resumé, stating when you may be available for work. Suggest a meeting when you arrive or beforehand, if practical.

Telephone calls

Telephone calls are intended to save time, but people often feel nervous when speaking. If you learn a few simple tactics before you pick up the phone, you will feel less anxious. Formulate your opening and closing remarks: identify yourself at the start, thank the other speaker for their time at the end. Clarify whom you want to speak to and the purpose of your call. What are you trying to discover or convey? Are you asking for information or help or an appointment? Write down exactly what you want to say, listen carefully to the answers. Have paper and pencil ready so you can take notes if necessary. Speak clearly – not too fast, not too loud. If you cannot hear clearly or need something spelt, ask for a repeat and – an easy tip – *smile* while you are talking. Smiling gives your voice a confident sounding lift. Find out who is in charge of recruitment as well as the name of the person you are speaking to, with their extension number, if any, and keep it for future reference.

What you need to know about the new location

You need to know as much as possible about the *general* job market in the new location. Both *domestic and international* job hunters should find out:

- the current job vacancy situation in the new area
- employment trends: expanding or contracting fields
- host location work restrictions, if any
- local limitations/assistance regarding self-employment
- local education/training opportunities and entry requirements
- current recruitment policy

Internationally, as Roger Jones points out in *How to Get a Job Abroad*, you must adjust to local conditions rather than attempt to 'recreate your own little England'. Working practices may vary considerably from those to which you are accustomed. It is essential to have a clear and accurate overall picture of the employment scene. You should also know about local working hours, holiday entitlements, language, commuting, health cover and similar areas. Consult Chapter 5, Marketing Yourself, for questions international career seekers should ask.

Working in a new location may involve a change of personal lifestyle. A move, for example, from the north to the south of England can bring unexpected surprises: different climate, transport facilities, pace of life, local attitudes and customs. Abroad, living conditions, health and safety concerns, friendships and socialising may be entirely different from those to which you, and your family, are accustomed. You are strongly advised to consider both lifestyle and career prospects together when contemplating moving far away from home.

International employment

Information about working overseas is rarely structured in a neat and tidy way. More likely, it will be fragmented, decentralised and disjointed. Compared to finding a job at home, it sometimes seems poorly communicated, difficult to research and closed to outsiders. There may be restrictions on the number of outsiders employers may engage, unless they are for specialist or short-term projects. A move abroad is more likely to be part of career development for existing employees seeking experience and promotion through in-house transfers and corporate postings.

As a non-resident, you should have something special to offer: an unusual technical skill, a qualification or competence in short supply, proven language competencies or prior travel experience to successfully break into the job market of the big multinationals and large corporations.

Sources of information about the new location

Domestic locations
Public libraries:
Your local branch library may have limited information resources. Go to a central reference library where you should find all UK and many international telephone directories as well as current professional directories, newspapers, magazines and journals. Ask for help when necessary.

Adult education centres
Business Information Network (gives details of regional business
  libraries
Confederation of British Industries (CBI)
Chambers of Commerce
Citizens' Advice Bureaux
Co-operative Development Agencies
Directories of charitable institutions
Directories of voluntary agencies

Employment agencies
Jobcentres and job clubs
National Franchise Association
Newspapers: national and local
Professional directories and year books
Recruitment consultants
Small Firms Advice
Specialist journals and magazines
Thomson Directories
Trade directories (*KOMPASS*)
University and college libraries
Yellow Pages

International locations
Public reference libraries (see above)
Host country embassy or consulate

Anglo – (host country) trade associations or similar
Briefing Centres
British Telecom International Enquiries: Dial 153
Business Information Network (gives details of business libraries)
Confederation of British Industries (CBI)
Chambers of Commerce
Directories of charitable institutions
Directories of voluntary agencies
FOCUS and similar resource groups
Foreign newspapers: national and local
International recruitment agencies
International magazines journals such as *The Economist*, *Newsweek*.
Jobcentres
Overseas clubs, societies, associations
Overseas editions of *The Times*, *Daily Telegraph*, etc.
Professional directories and year books
SEDOC (for EC jobs)
Specialist journals and magazines
Specialist books (eg TEFL, vacation work)
Trade directories (*KOMPASS*)

University and college libraries
Vacancy bulletins
Women's Corona Society
Women's network groups
Yellow Pages

The advertised job market

A large number of job-seekers concentrate on finding work from advertised job vacancies in the newspapers, professional and trade journals – at least as a starting point. It is easy to find which day is best for your type of work in the UK national press: the *Guardian*, for example, has an Education section every Tuesday, *The Times* has International vacancies on Fridays. Main public reference libraries carry copies of the daily newspapers and some trade journals.

In Britain, if you know where you are relocating, it is useful to read the local newspaper for several weeks before the move. This way, you gain inside knowledge about a place from reading about local issues, changes, amenities. Your own newsagent is usually helpful in finding out the best paper for the area you are interested in and will order it specially for you.

In general, foreign newspapers can be difficult to obtain and expensive to purchase in the UK, although some European dailies can be found in local shops. Helpful friends already resident in the required location may be able to send you suitable copies. University and business libraries (in London, the British Library Newspapers section and the London School of Economics) also carry selected newspapers, periodicals, professional and trade journals from abroad, but they rarely carry the latest editions. You do not have to be a registered student or academic: ask for 'Reading Only' facilities. For general information about newspapers, consult *Willing's Press Guide*, *Benn's Media Directory*, *Writers' and Artists' Yearbook*, *The Writer's Handbook*.

Responding to advertisements

Read advertisements very carefully indeed. Job vacancy announcements are *ideal* pictures, a description of the person the employer would *most* like to employ. The employer has a problem to solve, and this message represents his view of the ideal solution. Your task is to discover how closely you match those requirements and how best to convey that message.

Do not assume you cannot apply for jobs when you do not fit the advertisement exactly. There is a subtle difference between the employer's essential demands and those which are optional and less rigorous. Read the notice again and separate out the 'musts' ('driving licence essential') from the 'preferreds' ('should have sales experience'). After a while, you will see how some advertisements are far more flexible than others.

Individuals often worry about age limitations in job advertisements. Experts differ in their advice on this thorny topic: some say it is a complete waste of time to respond if you are outside the stated age band. Others say, provided you meet all the other requirements, three to five years before or beyond the preferred age is acceptable. And yet another view suggests that age issue should be ignored altogether, at least when first responding to the advertisement. You will find more on this topic in Chapter 8, also in Marketing Yourself, Chapter 5.

My advice is to consider the overall picture portrayed in the advertisement rather than limit yourself solely on one criterion such as age. Treat age in just the same way as other requirements in the classified listings: highlight any phrases, qualifications, skills and experiences mentioned that you are able to match and repeat these in both your CV and brief covering letter. Ignore those requirements which you are unable to fulfil. Covering letters are dealt with more fully in Chapter 5 (page 95).

The 'hidden' job market

The 'hidden' job market is often referred to but rarely explained. In general, it means those jobs which are obtained through word of mouth or through contacts. When a vacancy occurs, employers often chat to colleagues or trusted friends about finding a suitable individual to fill the post. Recruiters turn to agencies who have previously provided satisfactory staff; to school, college or club associates; to neighbours, acquaintances or relatives – anyone who they think may know of a good prospective employee. There is nothing necessarily devious about this; after all, a personal recommendation about practically anything is usually preferable to a complete shot in the dark. While these jobs may eventually be widely advertised in the press or by the personnel department, often there is a preferred candidate already discreetly earmarked by contact networks.

Networking

The reverse side of the 'hidden' job market for job applicants is networking. To 'network' is to talk to people about their jobs and ask for their advice. Networking means increasing your personal visibility to others who, in turn, may remember you when their own contacts invite potential candidates for job vacancies. Remember:

NETWORKING DOES NOT MEAN ASKING FOR A JOB

The idea of talking about work to any and every person you know may seem embarrassing at first. A first step is to chat casually to a neighbour about employment generally: what do they think about recent local redundancies, have they ever relocated to somewhere new, how did they get their first job and so on. Keep it general and low key.

Later, when your confidence has grown, talk or write to anyone you think may be in a position to give you information and advice. Whom should you approach? Many experts suggest making a list of everyone you have ever known in your life: school friends, past neighbours, previous business colleagues, professional advisers, ex-employers, community contacts, long lost relatives. Then identify those individuals who may be able to help. You may ask about:

- their own job: pros and cons
- how they obtained it
- future prospects in their field
- current recruitment practices (in general)
- names of others to whom you could refer for more advice

- their opinion of your CV
- employment prospects for spouses

If you are short of time, start with those who are closest to hand and most likely to produce a positive result: neighbours, friends, family, work mates, those with contacts in the new location or the same occupational field as yourself. A more leisurely approach includes networking with a wider spectrum of personal and professional contacts. The following ideas may be helpful for relocating partners, returners and those who have not been in continuous employment for some time. Many have an international membership and welcome enquiries from newcomers:

Community colleges, school associations
Enthusiasts clubs
European Women's Management Development Network
FOCUS Information Services
National Childbirth Trust
National Women's Register
Partners groups (military, foreign service, companies)
Professional institutes
Recreational and social organisations
Religious organisations
Rotary clubs
Royal British Legion
Specialised networks (in banking, engineering, publishing, etc.)
Sports clubs
Townswomen's Guild
UK Federation of Business and Professional Women
Universities, polytechnics
Veterans' associations
Voluntary organisations
Women's Institute

Information interviewing and cold calling
To set up an information interview, ask for a convenient time when you could have a chat with your contact for 20 or 30

minutes about your relocation and research on careers. Whenever possible, mention a mutual friend, or referral – the person who suggested the contact's name to you. Take along a notebook and pencil for jotting notes and details of further assistance; be punctual and smart; keep to the time allotted and remember to say thank you for the opportunity to meet. Be prepared to leave a copy of your CV if asked and always write a note of thanks afterwards.

Overview

- Do your homework about yourself. Gain the self-knowledge and confidence to market yourself effectively.
- Start with your present or recent employer for any help available.
- Attend meetings, briefing centres, workshops, seminars.
- Research information about the new location at a central public library.
- Write letters, telephone for information.
- Use business cards, especially in Japan.
- Target firms you are interested in, find named individuals to contact, gain informational interviews with contact persons.
- Talk to friends, neighbours, colleagues.
- Ask professional society/institute for foreign members' lists and write to them direct. Similarly, religious, academic, recreational, cultural and social organisations.
- Use recommended books and read them.
- Read the 'quality' newspapers at home and from the new location to discover employment/economic trends.
- *Begin the job search before you leave home.*

Selected books and information resources for international relocation

Australia

Books
Coyle, Wendy (1988) *On The Move*, Hampden Press, Sydney, Australia

Jones, Roger (1991) *How to Live and Work in Australia*, Northcote House, UK

Addresses
Australian High Commission, Australia House, Strand, London WC2 4LA (Also for Visa/Migration Enquiries)
Australian British Chamber of Commerce, 615 Linen Hall, Regent Street, London W1
Australian Department of Employment, Education and Training, PO Box 9880, Canberra ACT 2601
National Council of Overseas Skills Recognition (NCOSR), GPO Box 1407, Canberra ACT 2601

National Newspapers
The *Australian*
The *Australian Financial Review*

Belgium

Standard reference book
KOMPASS – Belgium

Address
British Council, British Embassy and British Chamber of Commerce: Britannia House, rue Joseph II 28, 1040 Brussels

National newspapers
Le Soir – Saturday edition
De Standaard – Saturday edition
Het Laatste Nieuws – Saturday edition, section 'Jobwijer'
De Gazet van Antwerpen – Saturday edition, section 'Top Job'

Denmark

Book
KOMPASS – Denmark

National newspaper
Politiken

European Community (general)

The SEDOC scheme is used for circulating EC vacancy information. It is normally operated by the Ministry of Labour in each country; it contains job vacancies and also job-seekers advertising themselves. Most countries expect foreigners to speak the language. Personal introductions and academic qualifications are helpful when searching for work. Job-seekers are frequently required to register with the police within a few days of arrival, and/or register for employment at local job centres. Even if you have already arranged a job, you should still check if registration is necessary and ask about work permit requirements.

Books

Raban, A J (1991) *Working in the European Community*, Office for Official Publications of the European Community, Hobsons Publishing PLC

Other publications include:

- *A Guide to Europe Without Frontiers* – mutual recognition (or otherwise) of professional qualifications
- *Directory of Higher Education Institutions*
- *European Community and recognition of diplomas for professional purposes*

For work in the EC Institutions and others with links to the Community, consult:

The European Communities' Yearbook, published annually in English, French and German, from Éditions Delta, 92–94 Square E. Palsky, B–1040 Brussels

France

Book
KOMPASS – France
France 30,000

National newspapers
Le Monde (monthly 'Campus' supplement)
Le Figaro

Address
Franco-British Chamber of Commerce: 8 Rue Cimarosa, 75016
  Paris

Germany

Book
KOMPAß – Deutschland

Address
British Chamber of Commerce: Heumarkt 14, Köhn 1

National newspapers
Die Welt – Saturday editions
Frankfurter Allegmeine Zeitung – Saturday and Wednesday
  editions
Süddeutsche Zeitung – Saturday editions
Handelsblatt (business jobs)
Job vacancy magazine: *Karriere*

Greece

Address
British Hellenic Chamber of Commerce: 4, Valaoritou Street
  106/71 Athens

National newspaper
Ta Nea – job advertisements Monday – Friday

Italy

Books
KOMPASS – Italy
Annual supplement to *Il Monde*

National newspapers
Corriere della Sera
La Repubblica

Address
British Chamber of Commerce: Corso Buenos Aires 77, 202124
Milan

Japan

Book
Brockman, T (1990) *The Job Hunter's Guide to Japan*, Kodansha
International, Tokyo and New York

Addresses
British Chamber of Commerce, Kowa 16 Bldg Annex, 9–10
Akasala, 1–chome, Minato-ku, Tokyo 107
Japanese Embassy, 101 Piccadilly, London W1 (also Consular
Visa and Information Section)
KAISHA Society (a non-profit organisation for non-Japanese
employees of Japanese corporations and institutions) c/o The
Press Club, Yurakucho Denki Building, 20th floor, 1-7-1
Yurakucho, Tokyo 100

National newspaper
The Japan Times

Netherlands (The)

Address
Netherlands – British Chamber of Commerce: Javastraat 96,
2585 The Hague

National newspapers
de Telegraaf
Algemeen Dagbla

Books
KOMPASS Netherlands
Intermediair Jaarboek (for graduates)

Portugal

Address
British – Portuguese Chamber of Commerce, Rue de Estrela 8,
  1200 Lisbon

National newspapers
Expresso job supplement is *Expresso Emprego*)
Jornal de Boticias
Anglo Portuguese News

Spain

Address
British Chamber of Commerce: Marques de Valdeiglas 3,
  Madrid 4.

Books
KOMPASS – España
5000 España

National newspaper
El Pais – weekend editions

United States of America

Book
Mills, Steve (1988) *How to Live and Work in America*,
  Northcote House, UK

Addresses
United States Embassy, 24 Grosvenor Gardens, London W1A
  2JB
  Visa Branch, 5 Upper Grosvenor Street, London 1A 2JB
    (Hotline 0891 200 290)
  Reference Centre: 071-499 9000, extension 2925
US/UK Educational Commission: 071-486 1631

British American Chamber of Commerce
   275 Madison Avenue, New York, NY 10016
   3150 California Street, San Francisco, CA 941115
Postgraduate Scholarships:
   US/UK Education Commission, 6 Porter Street, London
      W1A 2LH
   Fullbright Commission, 6 Porter Street, London W1M 2HR
   Thouron Awards, University of Glasgow, Glasgow G12 8QQ
   Kennedy Memorial Trust, 16 Great College Street, London
      SW1P 3RX
   Harkness Fellowships, 38 Upper Brook Street, London
      W1Y 1PE

US National newspapers
The Wall Street Journal
The Herald Tribune
USA To-day

(See also Useful Resources)

4. Employment on the Move

This chapter has four sections:

1. Flexible work that you can take up as a freelance or as an employee, part- or full time, as a breadwinner or, more likely if you are an accompanying partner, to supplement the family income and help maintain your career continuity.

2. Professional specialists on the move: where you may or may not be able to practise your profession directly, alongside some ideas about substitute work for non-practitioners.

3. Members of the Armed Forces who find themselves wondering which civilian jobs may be worth exploring after redundancy or resettlement.

4. A short selection of ideas for those retiring – early or on time – from paid work.

Your completed summary page from Chapter 2 (Table 2.4, page 33), will enable you to review the ideas contained here. Use the information broadly and consider all possible alternatives: try not to think only in terms of the *job title*, but ask yourself if the work fits into your employment plans, accumulated skills, new direction.

As a relocating partner, you need to be as flexible as possible to create employment opportunities, especially if you are in a high mobility situation. If, for example, you are accompanying an 'oil' spouse, you will probably move frequently to entirely different parts of the globe where, in some circumstances, your employment activity is restricted by local legislation. Then you must not only use skills acquired at home but also those acquired during each transfer and adapt them to the new territory on a recurring/cumulative basis. Your portable career could be in paid work, the volunteer section, as a foreign correspondent or teleworker – or all of them over the years.

This lifestyle differs greatly to a once-only transferee. If you are moving within Britain, the opportunities for career continuity are better. Despite regional variations, you will be familiar with the language, culture and social environment. Your employment opportunities will be relatively unrestricted, and your skills and plans stand a better chance of becoming fulfilled. Even so, you may not be able to find your ideal job at first. Flexibility and open-mindedness, therefore, are very desirable qualities for all portable career seekers.

Many portable careers offer a choice between self-employment, freelance work and working for an employer. This decision is for you, alone, to take, but remember to read the sections, Self-employment and Flexible patterns of work in Chapter 7.

The information below is correct at time of going to press. You are strongly advised to check current international requirements with appropriate officials at the relevant Embassy or High Commission, and with a professional Institute or Association to which you may have access.

Flexible work opportunities

Aid agencies

The major aid agencies, such as the United Nations, British Red Cross and Save the Children, usually send people overseas on medium-term contracts (two or three years). They look for qualified individuals, often in the medical, engineering, veterinary or teaching occupations. They are glad to receive enquiries from those made redundant or in resettlement situations, but may not have anything to offer relocating partners. Contact aid agencies before leaving home or make yourself known to local field workers when you arrive in the host country.

United Nations
The United Nations is a very large international employer with thousands of workers in locations around the world. It comprises six major central organisational units with various specialised agencies, committees, commissions and subsidiary bodies. There are permanent posts (specialists and other high-level personnel), general service posts (mostly support positions) and contract jobs, many of which are recruited by the Overseas Development Administration (ODA). Preferred applicants for most posts, apart from administrative support staff, are highly educated individuals having strong technical backgrounds, international experience and language competencies. Recruitment for the UN Secretariat takes place in New York. For information on job vacancies there, contact:

> United Nations
> Recruitment Programmes Section
> Office of Personnel Services
> New York
> NY 10017

Other UN departments such as International Court of Justice, International Labour Organisation, UN Children's Fund, UN Educational, Scientific and Cultural Organisation, World Bank and the World Health Organisation, are responsible for recruiting their own staff. In Britain, you can find information about these and other UN Departments from the UN Information Centre.

Arts administration
This category of work, usually involving the management of artists, theatres, orchestras, dance companies, can be used at several levels, in many environments. For example, there are huge arts complexes in city centres as well as small scale community groups. There are the international entrepreneurs as well as general factotums. Consider small, experimental dance groups or

local visual primitive art centres who are often desperate for administrative help; festival direction which is usually short-term but rewarding practical experience; international exchange schemes and competitions for young musicians, artists, dancers, etc; arranging funds, sponsorship and patronage are further options.

Useful information from: The Arts Council of Great Britain.

Assertiveness training
Assertiveness is one of the many life skills considered useful in dealing with others and living in society. It is usually taught in single sex group workshops with students of various ages. Formal qualifications are unnecessary for a place on a training course although experience of group work, especially with women, is an advantage; previous personal assertiveness training is also desirable. The Redwood Women's Training Association offers a Diploma and accreditation. Assertiveness courses may be attractive to business management schools, secondary and tertiary colleges, social service organisations and women's organisations. Contacts in these fields may be able to provide opportunities.

Useful information from: Redwood Women's Training Association.

Bed and breakfast
The traditional 'bed and breakfast' idea seem to have moved on from the old-fashioned dreary image to that of a smart and well-run service that is just as popular as ever. It has even travelled abroad: in the USA, home-based accommodation is often lavishly furnished (antiques are popular) and heavy with 'charm' and 'atmosphere'. Running a small guest house or B & B accommodation is a full-time job requiring stamina and versatility; marketing and financial skills are also necessary. If you intend to offer dinners as well, think about enrolling on a catering course. Contact local tourist boards, local companies, travel agents, airlines. Check local legislation beforehand.

Useful information from: The Hotel and Catering Training Company.

Business training

Business-related skills, such as entrepreneurial, communication, interpersonal, financial, marketing and negotiating skills, which are unusable directly, may be transferred to instructing others as a useful alternative. Such training sessions involve mostly group work with students and/or those aspiring to rise up the corporate ladder, but are also of interest to women, the self-employed and job-seekers. You must be able to communicate well with people of all abilities. Opportunities are to be found through personnel departments, business schools, tertiary colleges, voluntary organisations and missions.

More information: Try business schools and business studies courses at various colleges and polytechnics. They offer an interesting insight into the variety of skills required in business and business training.

Counsellor

Counsellors offer confidential short- or medium-term support and help to clients with personal or emotional problems. Some counsellors specialise in specific problem areas, such as drugs, alcohol, marital or family relationships. Mobility often incurs a high degree of stress with which counsellors may be able to assist; experience in helping teenagers and married couples may be especially useful.

Training is essential. Courses do not usually require formal qualifications but often ask for broad life experience, a non-judgemental attitude and sound common sense. In some countries (especially the USA), counsellors must be graduates and obtain a state licence: check first.

In Japanese culture there is reluctance to seek help, so very little market exists for counselling or psychology. However, at the time of writing, there are no restrictions or certification procedures for foreigners so it may be possible to create a market, possibly among foreign families, expatriates and business people, relating to marital, stress management, or alcohol related problems.

Useful information from: British Association for Counselling, which provides a Directory of Training in Counselling and Psychotherapy.

Crafts

Teaching others a practical skill that you, yourself, enjoy – at whatever level of attainment – can be a pleasure in itself. Expect students of very variable ability and of all ages. Most adult learners are strongly motivated and, thus, very rewarding to teach. Youngsters, on the other hand, are sometimes encouraged to take up craft work just to keep them out of mischief!

Craft teaching opportunities include hospitals, institutions, social service outlets (youth groups, centres for the elderly, etc), private clubs and business social centres. Formal training courses for art, craft and design teachers include City & Guilds Certificates, but an exhibition of your own work at a local hall or craft show may be just as useful. Many craftspeople and artists just *do* it. Membership of organisations such as The Embroiderer's Guild and similar are worth considering.

Selling your own craft work often starts at local markets and fund-raising events, progressing to larger, commercially-run trade and public fairs. You will have to pay for a stall, provide your own lighting and display materials, price goods and keep financial records. Transport is essential.

Useful information from: Local craft councils; local adult education centres and adult residential colleges.

Driving

Driving is popular with those who find themselves out of regular employment. They turn to mini-cab work, taxi driving, limousine chauffeuring for the transport of people, pets, parcels and so on. In the UK, taxi drivers must be licensed, so the work should not be considered as a short-term job. To qualify, trainees must be over 21 years of age, and pass tests that may take up to two years' training. They should have a clean driving record, no criminal history, and a good memory for city centres such as London. All drivers should ensure that they possess appropriate insurance cover. In the US different rules apply in different states, so check regulations very carefully indeed.

To become a UK driving instructor, you must hold a full driving licence for four years without any disqualification and must pass the Department of Transport's written and practical examinations.

Useful information from: Department of Transport.

Fashion

This category includes everything from textile design and manufacture to the design, production and sale of garments and accessories. Home-based work, such as tailoring and dressmaking, knitting and decorative work, has a reputation for low wages and long hours. But, if you enjoy it and can profit by 'hands-on' experience or inspiration from other lands, there are opportunities. Take care not to jeopardise the position of local workers who may depend on such occupations for their livelihood. Colour consultancy, where individuals receive advice about suitable colour schemes to suit their lifestyle, is a newer addition to the fashion business.

Useful information from: The Clothing and Footwear Industry.

Fitness instructor

Aerobics and similar fitness programmes are currently very popular. People come to expatriate sports clubs and centres for a wide range of activities, including some which are less athletic. Some business schools and corporate premises have on-site fitness centres; there may be opportunities in private clubs for exercise classes, rhythmic movement and remedial exercise sessions (eg back problems, sports injuries). Often, there are no specific qualifications apart from enthusiasm, but consider taking City & Guilds or BTEC courses.

Useful information from: Institute of Leisure and Amenity Management; Institute of Baths & Recreation Management.

Hospitality

Around the world, hotels and restaurants cater for the needs of business travellers and holidaymakers, while international fast food outlets have arrived even in the most remote locations. Growth is expected to continue as both business travel and tourism expand. Large hotel chains offer opportunities for direct transfers; in some smaller establishments, where one person directs all operations, experienced assistance may be welcomed. General hotel management is a portable career, as are food and beverage services, housekeeping management and front-of-house supervisors. Sandwich and lunch snacks are popular in many cities (particularly in Japan, so I am told); these may be sold either over-the-counter or delivered direct to offices. Check local health and safety regulations if you start up a home-based service.

Useful information from: Hotel and Catering Training Company; Hotel, Catering and Institutional Management Association.

Importing and exporting

Establishing a supply of products from one country and linking it to demand in another country is a well-established form of business. For the first-timer, there are financial risks and, inevitably, much paperwork: customs, shipping, taxes and so on. If you like this type of enterprise, it is better to work for somebody else before setting up on your own. Once you have learned the trading business, you need little more than a telephone, fax machine and a willing bank manager. Alternatively, you may prefer to become an import/export broker – negotiating price and introducing suppliers to purchasers without becoming involved in permits and red tape.

Useful information from: Department of Trade and Industry; trade associations of host countries.

Interior design/decorating

Although interior design is a recognised field in its own right, interior decorating links into many other crafts and service occupations. Designers generally have art school training and work for commercial organisations, with architects or as consultants. Interior decorators, on the other hand, do not necessarily have formal qualifications; they acquire experience over the years. Opportunities for work occur within expatriate communities and in private homes in the host country. Department stores, architects, specialist shops may be useful contacts for recommendations.

Useful information from: The Chartered Society of Designers; Interior Decorators and Designers Association Ltd.

Languages

The best jobs using foreign languages are for those who are fluent in an unusual language such as Japanese, Arabic or Russian. Other assets include a multi-lingual background and travel experience. Look for work in agencies, at conferences, with the media, industry or commerce and translation bureaux. A high level of proficiency is expected, plus literary, technical or scientific knowledge. If you wish to teach a foreign language, within Britain or overseas, consider offering your services as a tutor to individual students, to business people (who often want to learn everything very quickly!) and to local schools and colleges. Read the section below on qualifications and recognition for teaching and training (page 76).

Useful information from: The Institute of Linguists.

Music, drama and dance

Apart from the top few, most classical and popular instrumentalists, singers, dancers and stage workers find it hard to make a regular living anywhere in the world as solo performers. Many teach or coach others to supplement their income and this makes for a portable career. They also become accompanists, coaches or répétiteurs for instrumentalists, opera singers (amateur and professional) and choirs. In Japan, jazz musicians are especially popular; in the USA small live bands at hotels and restaurants attract customers. Overall, most locations have some access to choirs, and glee clubs; musical shows, folk and ethnic dancers; regional theatre and touring companies.

Active tuition may be offered to individuals; classwork with youth groups, amateurs, educational, training and exchange schemes. In addition, there are the related therapeutic fields, ie music therapy and psychodrama, and links into health and fitness (dance exercises, etc). Opportunities and contacts are found through arts administrators, agents, festival organisers, schools of music and drama, and examination boards. Various colleges of music and polytechnics offer long tuition to degree/professional level, but short courses are sometimes available for amateurs; look, too, at local adult education centres, adult residential short courses.

Additionally, consider the growth in cable and satellite television, videos, home movie rentals, local television and radio offering opportunities of work as a disc jockey, critic, librarian or just to gain visibility and experience in your specialism. For film work in the USA, it is usually necessary to register with a casting agency such as Central Casting, a no-fee agency that works with the Screen Extras Guild

Useful information from: Various schools of music, dance and drama. For details about therapy training, consult the British Association for Counselling.

Nutrition
Diet and nutrition experts have opportunities in hospitals, health and social work centres, hotels and catering outlets, schools, community groups, industrial research, food and welfare organisations, especially in developing countries. Special groups – the elderly, infants, diabetics and ethnic sectors – require dietary expertise as do slimming clubs, the fashion world and the media. British qualifications may not be recognised everywhere, so check before departure.

Useful information from: British Dietetic Association; Institute of Home Economics.

Office support services
As Joanna Foster implies in her afterword, girls were told to take up shorthand and typewriting because it would 'always come in useful'. These days, the most portable secretarial skills still require keyboard familiarity but the keyboard now connects to a word processor. Would-be mobile secretaries, bookkeepers and other administrative support staff should update on office technology

as the office revolution may be far more advanced in other countries. Learn database management, spreadsheet operations and word processing applications; familiarise yourself with fax machines, modems and networks; refresh your skills on switchboards, answering machines and so on. Seek job opportunities in business and commercial centres, with English-speaking firms, international organisations, voluntary bodies, and in trade and tourism, education and health. For some international jobs, such as with the Red Cross, you will need specific experience in addition to secretarial skills; telephone the London headquarters of international organisations for on-the-spot information.

Personal Care

This category includes hairdresser, barber, manicurist, beauty consultant (usually linked to a cosmetic company), chiropodist, masseur. Although many personal carers work in salons, others are self-employed with their own portable career. They travel to clients' homes, to hospitals, residential homes, day centres, hotels, social and sports clubs. Some work in department stores, airports, on passenger ships, in television and films. Because the work involves treating many different kinds of people, you should be adaptable and tactful, familiar with the out-of-fashion as well as the latest styles. Training and experience are necessary. To visit clients away from a salon, you require transport and your own equipment; abroad, make sure electrical items have the correct voltage; everywhere you need discretion, a sense of humour and patience.

Useful information from: City & Guilds of London Institute, BTEC.

Photography

Professional photographers usually train at art school or on recognised vocational courses, but talented amateurs also take family and individual portraits and, of course, wedding photographs. They sell to magazines, calendars, books, estate agents, schools, colleges, courts, insurance companies; there is a further area of work in photographing injuries for medical records. You must have your own equipment and transport. It is advisable to take recognised courses.

Useful information from: British Institute of Professional Photography.

Remedial cosmetics/cosmetic camouflage

This career should not be confused with beauty consultants, employed by cosmetic firms to demonstrate and sell their products. Cosmetic or remedial camouflage is used to hide birth marks, disfigurement or blemishes following accidents or plastic surgery. Usually, remedial cosmetics are taught as part of The International Beauty Therapist's Diploma, although training may be available through some voluntary bodies (eg Red Cross). Camouflage specialists work in hospitals, clinics and residential homes and alongside medical consultants. Opportunities may be found in state and independent medical establishments, specialist health and fitness centres and international charities.

Useful information from: The International Health and Beauty Council.

Sports coach

If you are dreaming about rushing off to Africa to work as a tiddlywinks coach, think again: certainly golf, tennis, football and swimming are international but other sports may have limited appeal. Enthusiasm is very desirable but a recognised coaching qualification is even better: contact sports governing bodies for course details. Training may also be obtained through professional experience, amateur activities such as local team membership, and short courses. Instructors require good communication skills, must like hard work and be physically fit, as well as being able to inspire confidence in others.

Useful information from: The Sports Council; National Coaching Foundation.

Teaching English as a foreign language (TEFL)

Teaching English as a foreign language is a popular portable career for all age groups and most life stages. There is a constant demand for learning English world-wide, particularly from business and professional people, and not enough qualified teachers. In practice, a recognised qualification is not necessary, but a Royal Society of Arts or Trinity College, London, certificate or diploma assists your marketability. Opportunities include one-to-one tutoring, group work, and formal classes in varied work settings (ie schools, colleges, missions, training departments). Students may be of all age groups and backgrounds.

Useful information from: EFL Careers Guide, from EFL Ltd.; also English Language Unit, The British Council.

Tourism

The travel and tourism industry is gigantic, but subject to fluctuations and fashion. Jobs created by these changes include accommodation and catering related services such as Hospitality and Bed and Breakfast (see pages 63 and 60), transport staff (airlines, railways, buses, ships, cars) and leisure services: tourist guides, couriers, resort representatives, museum and historic home staff, countryside and park staff, tourist information centre staff. Some of these jobs are seasonal and freelance, but if you enjoy working in a stately home and can stand hours on your feet, smiling at visitors, and also have at least one foreign language, there are opportunities for mature, friendly people with good memories, tact and diplomacy. Training for travel agents in handling reservations, tours and tickets is through courses approved by the Association of British Travel Agents (ABTA).

Useful information from: Association of British Travel Agents (send SAE).

Wine trade

Until recently, European wines, especially those from Germany and France, dominated the wine business. Now, as the consumption of wine has rocketed in Britain, wines from all over the world can be found in supermarkets and neighbourhood stores. If you fancy yourself as something of a wine connoisseur, preferably with languages as well, you may feel competent enough to tackle independent growers or small specialist vineyards with a view to selling their products at home or to your host community, subject of course to any local restrictions. Note the remarks on Importing and Exporting (page 64) before trading across frontiers. You could sell to hotels and restaurants, open your own wine bar (check legislation) take up viniculture yourself, or just enjoy the social status of a wine expert. Classes are available at many local adult education colleges; the Wine and Spirit Education Trust also offer individual home study as well as certificated courses.

Useful information from: The Wine and Spirit Education Trust (send SAE).

Working with animals

To work with animals, you must be fond of them but unsentimental. Jobs may be found as dog-walkers, or cat-sitters (parrot-sitters are not uncommon!) by advertising in the local press or shop windows. Or look after people's pets in your own home, subject to local regulations. Canine beauticians trim, wash and groom dogs (sometimes cats) either in shop premises or the home. There are futher opportunities in academic or industrial laboratories where animal technicians clean, feed and tend caged animals, probably rats or monkeys. Kennel work involves looking after racing or hunting dogs, animals in quarantine, breeding and boarding. To set up your own kennels or cattery, formal qualifications are unnecessary but you must have plenty of stamina, suitable premises and local authority consent. Veterinary nursing training takes two years, usually on a part-time basis. The work is a mixture of secretarial, kennel maid, surgical theatre assistant and care of post-operative animals. Opportunities may be found through animal welfare organisations and wildlife associations, as well as veterinary practices.

Another area of opportunity is fish farming. Trout, salmon and oysters are farmed intensively in areas where conditions are right and there is a good demand for the products. Apart from taking agricultural college courses, you need business related skills and practical experience of work as an assistant. Jobs with zoo animals – private or state run – are specialised and scarce, although there may be occasional conservation, modernisation and restoration work with animals' quarters, zoo buildings and visitor facilities.

Useful information from: British Veterinary Nursing Association.

Wedding and other organisers

A glance through the Yellow Pages almost everywhere in the English-speaking world will uncover a vast range of service people who organise just about anything for anybody in homes, offices and communities. For example, there are American 'Closet Organisers', who tidy drawers and cupboards leaving immaculately arranged books, papers, bed linen, utensils, clothing, etc; wedding and party organisers who take care of the details of caterers, florists, entertainers, dressmakers and so on; also relocation organisers, who – alongside or in addition to major firms – take on invaluable extra personal services to make a move smooth running and trouble-free. Jobs usually come about through recommendation; clients from companies are also possible. No known formal training, but imagination, a flair for self-marketing and an eye for detail seem essential.

Useful information: Talk to someone else who has done it themselves or employed a satisfactory service.

Writing and journalism

Writers require very little equipment or capital to start with, but take a long time to make any money! The old advice about reading as much as possible and only writing what you know about is still true today. Try acting as a correspondent while you are away from home for your network magazine, in-house journal or newsletter, as well as contributing technical reports, studies or surveys. Also, write about home for the local press. Several women with long experience of overseas travel and high mobility have published books about their experiences. Learn how to prepare an initial non-fiction book proposal and how to submit work. The fiction market – short stories and books – has always been difficult to break into; aspiring authors should expect many rejection slips before the magical acceptance arrives.

Useful information from: Writers' and Artists' Year Book and *The Writer's Handbook* (annual publications).

Yoga, Shiatsu, Alexander Technique instructor

Yoga teaching often provides a useful outlet for those wishing to keep flexible and in trim. Shiatsu is a massage-style acupressure technique linked to Eastern physiotherapeutic methods. Alexander Technique teachers help clients to use their bodies more efficiently in either one-to-one sessions or group work. None are instant pathways to great riches; opportunities are limited but may be personally satisfying and beneficial to participants. Contact local doctors, health and sports centres, and business fitness programmes for teaching opportunities. Training may take two years or more providing sessions requires suitable premises and some equipment.

Useful information from: Iyengar Yoga Institute; (Shiatsu) East/West Centre; Society of Teachers of Alexander Technique.

Professional specialists abroad

Professional specialists are often the most difficult to relocate. Lawyers, accountants, stockbrokers and similarly highly qualified professionals may not be permitted to practise directly in other countries without taking further licensing examinations, although there may be limited opportunities for some services depending on the location. Consider direct in-house transfers as your first choice. If unavailable, look for consultancy type services, a complete change or acquiring further skills to complement your experience. Always consult your destination Embassy or Consulate prior to leaving the UK and your own professional society, institute or association.

Accountancy

Direct, in-house transfers are best for qualified accountants wishing to remain in professional practice. Otherwise it may be difficult to transfer to a foreign accountancy firm. In most US states, Certified Public Accountants (CPA) are the only accountants licensed and recognised. Alternatively, consider working outside professional practice for a period as a financial or tax expert employed in business or industry, or tutoring in business schools; with charitable institutions, as an internal company auditor, or in management, sales, recruitment or training.

Transferable skills
Many business-related competencies – financial analysis, record-keeping, designing systems, auditing, advising, cash management, stock control, taxation, budgeting, etc – which you may be able to use on a business or management consultancy basis, in corporate settings, finance houses, insurance or small business advice settings.

Architecture
Demand for architects fluctuates according to economic changes in most parts of the world. British credentials are not automatically recognised everywhere: qualified nationals are permitted to work in the EC but UK professionals are only 'recommended' by Commonwealth and Middle East countries. US states require individuals to be licensed prior to setting up in practice. Employment is possible without registration, but only a licensed architect has legal responsibility for the work. Working and on-site living conditions abroad are very variable; many construction jobs are for singles only.

Transferable skills
Business acumen, creativity, mathematical and drawing ability, visual resources, accuracy, technical know-how and communication skills.

Banking and finance
Both these fields have experienced a growing internationalisation, nevertheless, professional bankers need a direct transfer. In Japan, you are unlikely to get a job unless already employed by an

international bank and it is essential to speak the language and understand the culture. Without a direct transfer, there are only slim chances of employment even if you speak Japanese proficiently, have excellent quantitative skills and a specialism. Your other options include linking into other numeracy-based occupations (accountancy, insurance, etc) or moving away from the financial side towards promoting bank services, personnel recruitment, sales, staff development.

Engineers

Usually there are many openings, but if not, try teaching (maths, design principles), research and development companies, sales, consultancy, building management or surveying. Production and sales are also possible.

Health care – an overview

It is essential to check if your medical qualifications are recognised in a foreign destination. Although British qualifications are widely respected, many countries, including the USA, require you to take further examinations before you are permitted to practise. UK Registered General Nursing (RGN) qualifications are recognised in the European Community. In developing countries, nursing posts generally require both RGN and RM (midwifery) qualifications; Enrolled Nursing (EN) status is less commonly recognised, although ENs work in some Commonwealth countries as aides and assistants and sometimes in the USA, Europe, Middle East and Asia. But, most of these countries ask for RGN plus a specialist qualification.

Some medical workers travel abroad on an emergency basis only and in response to disasters; others work on longer-term contracts, but only within their own specialism, in conditions which may be primitive and difficult. Be prepared!

General practice

For those unable to practise directly, there are usually opportunities in public health appointments, voluntary organisations, international charities and missions, industrial projects, construction sites, drug companies, and occupational and environmental groups. Expatriate communities with their own medical facilities welcome British and/or American professionals.

Nursing

Midwifery opportunities are good in Europe, the Commonwealth and Third World as are geriatric, intensive care and drugs clinic specialisms. Languages and a flexible outlook are useful as it may be necessary to adapt to an entirely different way of life and working practices.

Volunteer work includes postings with mission hospitals and dispensaries where nurses provide curative, preventative care and follow-up medicine; educational work at nutrition classes with local schools and relief work in emergency situations, although this is usually only at very short notice. Paid work opportunities may be available through aid agencies, overseas government agencies, industrial and commercial concerns or private recruitment agencies.

Alternatives to traditional nursing include school, military, prison and industrial nursing; work with elderly, psychiatric, disabled and disadvantaged people. Nurses may turn to teaching, either within the profession, in special schools and establishments or to a wider spectrum of people – with such topics as health education, dietetics, hygiene, fitness and well-being. Related careers include: therapy work (music, art, counselling); health visiting, social work and industrial nursing.

Allied professions

Dentists can usually work in the Commonwealth and EC. *Radiographers* may need languages. *Physiotherapists:* for US employment, more qualifications are necessary. *Osteopaths:* good opportunities are available as there is a world shortage at present.

Law

It is usually very hard for lawyers to be transferred to other countries unless they obtain work directly with an international firm. Some limited opportunities exist in the Commonwealth but not in the European Community, USA or Middle East. In Japan, only lawyers from those countries granting equal treatment to Japanese lawyers are licensed and, once registered, foreigners may provide only a narrow range of services, usually related to business matters.

Specialists in tax or patents may be able to work with engineering, science or accountancy firms; others may wish to acquire a new field of expertise. Non-practising lawyers may coach students for UK qualifications, advise expatriates or corporations, or deal with business, money, trade or property related contracts. Legal training is useful in other areas such as business management, journalism, politics, security and industrial arbitration.

Transferable skills
Communication, analysis, negotiation, problem-solving, research and information, and decision-making skills.

Scientists
UK researchers are often sought by foreign employers. In Japan, both private sector and foreign companies seek foreign experts in specific industries. They prefer those aged between 25 and 45. There are language difficulties and situational differences: big rooms, no private office, little quiet, a six-day week with long hours and few holidays.

Teaching and training
Education and training skills are among the most portable careers for almost anywhere in the world, but make sure your British qualifications are acceptable. EC, US and Canadian *state* schools are unlikely to accept British qualifications; instead, think about working in the independent sector. Always contact and check with the relevant Embassy or Consulate. Enquire, too, if they will send you a list of educational establishments where tuition is in English or a British curriculum operates. (For TEFL see previous section page 68.)

Transferable skills
Apart from their specialist subject knowledge – English, history,

geography, etc – most teachers possess a very wide range of transferable skills including:

Making oral presentations, writing, giving instruction, stimulating and fostering people's learning, articulating and explaining, demonstrating, group-facilitating, encouraging and helping, public speaking, time management, committee collaboration, operating machinery, manual dexterity, fixing equipment, record-keeping, researching, reasoning, analysing, collating, evaluating, planning and administering, monitoring, costing, checking.

There are teaching opportunities with most age groups and in many subjects and settings. If you possess a specialist knowledge – in practical, technical, business or recreational as well as academic and language fields – you may be able to offer instruction at either formal or informal levels. Opportunities may exist for instructing groups with special needs – the handicapped, disabled, disadvantaged, the very young or elderly.

Outside mainstream teaching, consider openings as activity leaders, supervisors and instructors with young people's holiday companies, language schools or shipping lines. For teachers with adult education experience, the increasing number of Summer Schools and Educational Tours offer openings. International voluntary bodies sometimes have openings for both specialist and general teachers.

Teachers can become writers, desk top publishers, press critics, therapists, educational advisers; turn to youth work, community programmes, leisure management, health education, counselling and career advisory services. Some take up administration, publishing, museum education and media (radio, TV, video) projects.

A move into skill training with adults, either freelance or in direct employment, is another possibility. Some skills are trade and industry specific – plumbing, electrical, etc – but others concern youth and adult development, people with specific needs (women, minority, ethnic groups) and management enhancement programmes. Training topics include interpersonal skills, team interaction, creative thinking, public speaking, decision making, problem solving, negotiation and conflict resolution.

A few general points about teaching and training:

- Whenever possible, obtain employment, even a short-term contract, before leaving home. Building upon temporary work is easier than cold calling.

- Teaching experience is desirable, but not always essential. As Susan Griffiths points out in *Teaching English Abroad*, most establishments look for teachers 'with a good educational background, clear correct speech, familiarity with the main issues and approaches . . . and an outgoing personality'. These are realistic and constructive remarks that apply to all portable career seekers, not solely to TEFL teachers.

- Formal qualifications do not always guarantee employment. What you must have, however, are reliable and reputable credentials. Pack copies of your personal references, college certificates, press cuttings and similar for potential local employers' inspection. Don't set yourself up as an expert if you can't prove it!

- Take care to understand that learning differs from country to country. Some students, for example, are accustomed to learning by rote, others use a learning-by-doing approach.

- For traditional teaching opportunities *abroad*, contact The British Council, Medlock Street, Manchester M15 4PR (061-957 7000). Advertisements for teaching opportunities appear in the British national press regularly, especially in *The Times Educational Supplement* and *The Times Higher Education Supplement*.

What else can a soldier do?

Military personnel hold a vast range of different jobs: managerial, administrative, professional, technical, clerical, construction, electrical, electronic, mechanical, repair and so on. For much of the following information, I am indebted to The United States Department of Labor Occupational Outlook Handbook Guide (1990–91). They suggest that 'over 75 per cent of these occupational specialities have civilian counterparts'. For those in the British Armed Forces facing a return to civilian life or for others who find themselves redundant, which work environments and jobs are worth exploring?

Work environments

Life in the Armed Forces is more regimented than civilian life, with stringent dress, grooming, social and work requirements. Planning a return to civilian life involves not just finding a job, but adjusting to an entirely different lifestyle where employment, among other matters, is less dependent on rules, formalities, obedience or conforming to authority. Before you decide which job may be related to the civilian counterpart, consider the following.

Structured work environments are usually found in large organisations such as state institutions, the Civil Service, local authorities, large public companies, banks, etc. There is often a clearly defined, orderly, task-orientated management over staff who respect the rules while they get the job done. Promotion, salary increases, holidays and workaday life are often predictable; jobs are achieved steadily and on schedule; detail, accuracy and care are valued and the best employees are reliable and stable with consistent performance. There follow some examples of employers who traditionally have had structured working environments. You should note, however, that many have or are about to change with decentralisation and privatisation. Nevertheless, you may wish to think about organisations such as:

Airport authorities
Air traffic control
Ambulance services
Customs and Excise
Fire Service
Environmental Health Departments
Port authorities
Hospital administration
Inspectorates (Quarries, Factories, Mines)
National Trust

NSPCC, RSPCA
Prison staff
River authorities
Schools, universities and colleges
Security services
Trading Standard Departments
Transport services

An example of a more *relaxed work climate* would be a research and development company. R & D employees are expected to come up with new ideas, challenge the rules, generate innovative dynamics and solve problems in unexpected ways. Staff here are individualistic, entrepreneurial, flexible and ideas-orientated. They enjoy using their versatility, like variety and change, and enjoy the challenge to do things differently. Similarly, smaller firms are often less rigid, with employees doing whatever needs to be done regardless of whose job it actually is. Such less regimented working environments are also to be found in advertising agencies, the entertainment business, some aspects of social work and journalism.

Transferring to a civilian career

There are two important questions to consider when you want to use the skills learned through military training in civilian employment. First, what are the prospects for the job or job family for which you possess existing skills? Are these prospects good or poor? Is it a growth industry or in decline? Second, are your qualifications adequate for the civilian workplace? Do you need more? If your answer is 'yes', you need to know what additional training is required, where it may be obtained, how long it will take. For answers to these questions, consult your resettlement office and any of the career books mentioned in Chapter 3.

Many military personnel transfer directly into the civilian sector ie: medical, dental and health professions; electrical, electronic equipment and mechanical equipment repair occupations; musicians, photographers, graphic designers; carpenters, heating, plumbing and construction operators. Others, such as functional support and administration staff, turn their skills to computer programming, bookkeeping, personnel management, or storekeeping. Communications and intelligence specialists move into air traffic control, radio and radar operations.

There are some functions which are unique to the armed forces – infantry, gunners, weapons specialists. Some may involve skills that can be applied to a number of civilian occupations such as police and security services, firefighting, heavy equipment operators and so on (as listed above). It is worth remembering that, even if you cannot transfer directly from one of these jobs into a civilian counterpart, you are also skilled at working as a team member and can develop leadership, managerial and supervisory skills.

Useful resources: Soldiers', Sailors' and Airmen's Families Association/Forces Help Society (SSAFA/FHS), The Royal British Legion.

Jobs and careers for those with few or no formal qualifications
Even if you have only one paper qualification or none at all, there are jobs and careers available to you and some may also include a training programme, day release or in-house apprenticeship. Many jobs require you to have simple numeracy (addition, subtraction, multiplication, division) to work out money or measure accurately; in others you will need to be able to spell, write and read easily. If these are not your strongest skills, consider practical abilities: working machines, making things, decorating, gardening, car repairs. Ask yourself where your preferences lie: do you work well by yourself and enjoy getting on with the job? Are you a good timekeeper, do you get along with all sorts of people, do you mind getting dirty, are you fit and physically strong? Are you patient, single-minded, have a clear speaking voice, keen on fashion, calm, able to do fiddly tasks? These are all transferable qualities for which jobs do exist, jobs with people, in offices, outdoors, in practical and general services. (For helpful books, see the 'Useful Resources' section.)

Resources for those retiring from paid work – early or on time

Employment/voluntary work

Retired Executive Action Clearing House links volunteers to organisations in need. REACH, 89 Southward Street, London SE1 0HD; 071-928 0452

Success After Sixty, 40–41 Old Bond Street, London W1X 3AF; 071-629 0672

National Association for Voluntary Organisations, 26 Bedford Square, London WC1B 3HU; 071-636 4066

Maturity may be valued by firms linked to:
Financial advice
Friendship and companionship
Gardening
Handicrafts
Heritage
Leisure pursuits (bridge, chess, etc)
Mobility
Pets/animals
Religious groups
Safety
Sport (golf/ bowls, etc)
Travel and holidays for older age groups
Well-being, health and fitness

Education
Local Adult Education Authorities
Open University
Open College

National Institute of Adult Continuing Education represents the interests of everyone concerned with adult learning. Courses (weekend or longer) to suit all levels of experience at many residential centres listed in *Time to Learn*, issued twice yearly. NIACE, 19b de Montfort Street, Leicester LE1 7GE.

University of the Third Age is a self-help association of men and women who participate together in study and social experiences to enhance their quality of life. Open to any retired or unemployed person, without age limits or entry tests. U3A c/o BASSAC, 13 Stockwell Road, London SW9 9AU (also try your local library for nearby U3A groups).

Workers' Educational Association, 9 Upper Berkeley Street, London W1H 8BY; 071-402 5608.

National groups
The Association for Retired Persons represents the over-50s, and aims to enhance the quality and purpose of life for those retired or planning retirement throughout the United Kingdom. Regional, county and local groups are active with social and lobbying projects, including issues concerning ageism at work. ARP, 5th Floor, Hill House, Highgate Hill, London N19 5UY.

Kogan Page books
The Mid Career Action Guide, 2nd edition, Derek Kemp and Fred Kemp
The Good Retirement Guide, 6th edition, Rosemary Brown (published annually)

(For further discussion of the issue of age and work, see also Chapter 8.)

5. Marketing Yourself

The subtle art of marketing your skills and experience has special significance for portable careers. 'How can I cover the gaps?' ask transferees 'I'm capable, reliable, mature, experienced, but how do I convey the message effectively if my work history is fragmented and inconsistent? As Joanna Foster noted in her speech to the CBI Employee Relocation Council (see Afterword, page 141), a 'stop–start patchwork' is a fairly typical career pattern for relocated partners.

The marketing of *you* can be compared to the sales campaign of any product or service. Imagine for a moment how you, as a consumer, decide to purchase a new product: did others recommend it? Is it attractively displayed? What are its advantages? In what way is it better than similar products? And, would you buy it if it had dull wrapping, illegible printing and offered no clear idea how it will solve your problems?

Your personal sales campaign is a sales campaign centred on *you*. Every job vacancy means the employer has a problem to solve and you could be the solution. In marketing yourself, you must increase your visibility, generate interest in your advantages and package your skills convincingly. CVs or résumés should communicate the message: 'Employer, you simply cannot afford not to interview me!' Your written efforts are appetising morsels – not full-blown meals – aimed at gaining an *interview*, not a job. They are positive, confident, assertive packages which state, loud and clear, how well *you* are able to solve the employer's problem.

When you apply for work, you become your own promoter,

image-maker, advertising agent and PR person all rolled into one. Selling yourself at a distance needs some hard thinking and concentrated work to overcome the obstacles, but skilled written and verbal communication demonstrating confidence and assurance will compensate over and over again for an employment history full of job changes and work gaps.

Know your own resources

To market yourself effectively you must know your own resources. If you are starting the job hunt with this chapter, please stop here. Do you know, in detail:

- What you have done with your life?
- What knowledge you possess?
- Your special qualities, personal reasons relating to the job?
- All your paid and non-paid work?
- Your achievements and special know-how?
- Your restraints and potential pitfalls?

If you answer 'No' to any of these questions, return to the self-assessment exercises in Chapter 2 and complete them (page 19). Taking stock of your own resources will help you to create a core of quality self-marketing material. If this task is proving difficult, take a CV workshop, join a job club or enlist professional help.

Presenting yourself attractively on paper

You will need to complete one or more of the following: a curriculum vitae (CV or 'track record'), a résumé, personal dossier, biodata form, a profile or 'biog' or a job application form.

- *A curriculum vitae, CV or 'track record':* In the UK the most acceptable way of presenting yourself is a brief record of your working life. The presentation is factual, objective and crisp.
- *A résumé:* A more variable account of your experience; style and quantity of information depends on the kind of job in view. Sometimes headed by an 'Employment Goal' or

'Objective', tailored to fit specific job openings. Usual in USA, Australia.

- *Personal dossier:* A highly detailed breakdown of many aspects of your life, including employment, education, personal data, testimonials, etc. Sometimes required for jobs abroad.
- A *profile or 'biog':* Usually a one page piece of prose, written in the third person, briefly describing major highlights of an individual's career/life. Like an elaborate calling card, it may be sent to or left with contacts or meetings to provide further individual information or avoid long-winded verbal life histories.
- *Job application forms:* Some simply require outline facts while others are general purpose personnel forms, possibly several pages long. Standard application forms (SAF) are more predictable than employer application forms (EAF), specifically designed to fit an organisation's own requirements.
- *Biodata forms:* These are designed by organisations to match employees to job profiles. Superficially, the forms are straight-forward: a list of questions is provided, each with several answers from which you must choose one response only. Less obviously, biodata forms are carefully constructed by specialists. Experts say it is not in your interest to answer dishonestly!

Written applications for portable careers

There are very many books and leaflets available to help you write up a CV, résumé or similar. Most advise you to create a general, one page 'core' CV that can be adapted for each new job application. It should contain well-organised information to show you in the best possible light and be directly relevant to the job vacancy. These are sensible recommendations, but you always should bear in mind there is no such thing as a 'perfect' CV or one which will guarantee you a place at a selection interview. In addition, portable careers have special problems, including:

- A fragmented work history
- A mono-track or over-specialised work history
- There may be gaps in your employment record

- You may have worked without pay for some time
- Employers may be unfamiliar with or wary about foreign firms
- It may look as if you cannot settle down or have opted out
- Age, dependants, spouses may appear too complicated
- Foreign qualifications are unfamiliar
- You appear to be underqualified or overqualified

Adjusting your written presentations for portable careers

To overcome some of the application problems of marketing yourself for a portable career, you can:

- Make life easier for recruiters by presenting easy-to-read material
- Offer equivalents for unfamiliar experience or qualifications
- Review CV or résumé formats and choose an appropriate one
- Use language employers understand
- Use covering letters to expand or clarify applications

Presenting easy-to-read material

Always bear in mind that your purpose in presenting written application material is *to gain an interview*. The recruiter must be able to *read* it. The following are essential:

- Good quality paper
- Typewriter or word processor
- Good, clear photocopying
- Capitals, underlining, bold print used sparingly
- Correct spelling and punctuation; check over and over again!

The *contents* should present true, concrete information about you in note form, highlighting your special assets and stressing the benefits of employing *you*. Recruiters do not like wasting time, particularly if an application for a job is speculative. They look for consistency and familiarity in layout and content. You can advantage yourself by knowing what to include.

In Britain, a CV will generally contain:

Heading. Accurate personal details including your name, address, correct postcode, telephone (home and work) and Fax numbers with dialling codes. Optional items: nationality, sex, marital status, availability dates. (Details of age and date of birth are commonplace in some countries, illegal in others: see Chapter 8.)

Work experience. State the names of previous employers, their location if relevant, your job title and responsibilities. Begin with your most recent or best experience. Concentrate on what *you* achieved rather than listing your responsibilities straight from the job description.

Publications/presentations. For academics this is an essential item. Others should consider the job-relevance of such information: ask yourself if it enhances your personal qualities or skill evidence for the vacancy.

Education. Include the knowledge you possess – training, education, courses, workshops – linked to the job. Leave out any irrelevant courses and any more than 15 years old unless they are highly pertinent. Course units taken during degrees, etc, should be included only by younger applicants seeking to expand their information. State where your knowledge was obtained and include local equivalents if necessary. If you do not know them, read the section below, Unfamiliar experience or qualifications.

Additional skills. This is the section where further job-relevant skills may be included, such as driving, computer literacy, languages (state proficiency level).

Interests. Keep this brief and to the point. Recruiters tend to be interested in team activities, fitness and leadership qualities. Omit hobbies or interests which are not linked to the field of work.

Special circumstances. State if you need or possess a work permit. Outline here anything to do with physical ability, health or other special circumstance. Offer a sentence or two about your future plans if your previous employment history has been very fragmented.

References. Never give referees' names without asking them first. Usually two or more are required, one of which may be a personal reference. Give full styles and titles, and accurate contact details. For speculative applications, it is acceptable to write 'References Available'.

Finally, check you have made your application as straightforward as possible for the recruiter. Polish your CV by checking over basic spelling, layout and approach. Ask yourself if it is understandable, coherent, factual. Is it tailor-made for you? Does it do you justice?

The USA résumé

A one or two page typed résumé; brief and accurate (no spelling or punctuation errors), confident language emphasising achievements and accomplishments. Academic details start with the highest degree and work backwards thus: degree, institution, major, date. Include significant academic honours. State one specific résumé objective or employment goal immediately underneath your personal details.

The Australian résumé

Similar to the US résumé style, but not too brief or poster-like. Attach a copy of the official transcript of academic results; include team sport activities whenever possible; indicate professional objective, aims, plans. Optional extra: passport-size photograph (flattering!) glued to the top right-hand corner.

Other countries

Ideally, one or two clean, typed pages, although some countries (check with relevant officials) require a dossier-sized document. Summarise schools/colleges, academic achievements, work history together with locations. Include publications, presentations, awards from civic, professional and volunteer experience. Not all countries want know about interests, hobbies and leisure activities. Mention current passport/visas, fluent languages and time spent abroad. State, in a short sentence, why you want to work in that country.

Application forms

You may be asked to complete an application form and return it to the organisation before candidates are selected for interview.

Some companies, mostly in the USA, short-list prospective interviewees first and then send a company application form which you are required to complete before interview.

Whenever possible, take two copies of any application form before writing a single word upon it. Use the copies to draft your answers so that the final version – the one you return to the company – is error-free, legible and accurate.

Read all the questions carefully. Some will be factual, others less exact. Refer to the job advertisement to link your answers to the employer's needs. Do not attempt replies which cannot be substantiated. If you have a lot to say about a certain topic, continue on to an additional page and attach it at the appropriate place. But do not expect the reader to plough through reams of your personal views and history. If there are questions you do not wish to answer, draw a line through the section of the form or write 'see accompanying letter' or 'N/A' (not applicable). Be prepared, however, to explain your action at interview.

Try to complete every section, bearing in mind the application form will (a) be the basis of your interview and (b) if you are selected, probably go on your Personnel Record with the company. Use clear handwriting in dark ink for filling in these forms unless yours is thoroughly unreadable when capital letters or typing will suffice.

Take a copy of the completed form before posting and check everything, including any accompanying letter, is included in the envelope.

Unfamiliar experience or qualifications

Some of you may have foreign qualifications or titles, or experience in occupations and organisations with which future employers may not be familiar. Don't expect the recruiter to know what every long string of initials means, or have in-depth knowledge of Messrs XYZ, Outer Mongolia, or about a PhD from an obscure college. Make life easier for the reader: include a short note alongside the relevant item and show an equivalent qualification or comparative experience.

If you want to know what your foreign qualification is worth in the UK, contact the National Academic Recognition

Information Centre for the United Kingdom, British Council. For information on recognition of British qualifications in overseas countries, contact the appropriate embassy.

CV or résumé formats
Which CV or résumé format will best suit your past experience and match the expectations of the prospective employer?

Chronological
UK employers are most familiar with this style of skeletal CV. It provides the 'bare bones' of your educational and employment history in chronological order, beginning with education and qualifications, continuing with previous work history in date order, and ending with referees. Sometimes there is a short section on additonal skills or interests and hobbies, occasionally salary is mentioned. The most usual size is one or two (at most) A4 pages.

Comment. The chronological approach emphasises work gaps because of the reminders of time and dates, but it is popular and familiar with employers. A well-presented, chronological CV will not usually go straight into the waste-paper basket, but it could land there just the same when career interruptions are noticed.

Functional
Here, brief summaries of skills and experience are presented under theme headings which concentrate more on interests and achievements. Your information is reorganised under headings such as Commercial Sense, Administrative Abilities, Communication Skills. Headings are related to the kind of work you want: for a managerial application, for example, you might want to show supervision, administrative, organisational and planning skills. Factual evidence is presented under each section and usually includes short, clear details of date, employers, job description and duration of work.

Comment. The functional CV does not emphasise specific dates and may well camouflage an interrupted record. It is ideal for those with career gaps, particularly returners, but the business world is not yet accustomed to a functional CV and recruiters tend to be suspicious of it.

Mixed/combination

The combination style provides employment history clustered or arranged under two or three general headings. A chronological work history section is sometimes given separately but, if you wish, employment dates may be omitted. There is a wider range of categories available. You can invent your own or try:

- Present/previously
- Organisational experience/personal skills
- Major work experience/additional information
- Times zones, eg: pre-1975/1975–85/post 1985
- Geographic areas, eg: UK/USA/EC/Third World

Comment. The mixed or combination CV format gives great flexibility by containing all the usual ingredients but without making interruptions obvious. It needs great care in layout to avoid becoming too long and boring. Employers who are unfamiliar with this approach may wonder what it hides.

Choosing a CV or résumé format

Your choice will depend on your personal work and non-work history, relevant experience and the recruiter you are addressing. If you have a fragmented employment history, with periods in paid work as well as time out of employment or in the non-paid, voluntary sector, the mixed or combination style is probably best. Group or cluster your employment record under suitable 'theme' headings and include significant unpaid experience as well as paid work.

For those with a mono-track career, one occupational field or area, the chronological format has many advantages. Here you can show the range of your experience, with different departments or employers. Take care not to sound too narrow or rigid: expand your personal qualities, interests or leisure pursuits to show you are an all-rounder with specialist experience.

If you may have worked without pay for some time, because of domestic responsibilities, foreign work restrictions or redundancy, the functional, mixed or combination styles are most likely to enhance your information. Treat non-paid experience as regular employment. Also include:

- Anything linked to financial or numerical targets/turnover (how many people did you manage, what size funds raised, how soon targets reached)
- Any recent prizes, awards, special recognition (academic, professional, civic, etc)
- Any relevant courses, updating, seminars, conferences, workshops attended
- Expected achievements – example: 'Degree expected Summer, 1993'
- Keep-in-touch schemes, professional journals and memberships
- Course contents if relevant to job and only if presently studying.

Use language employers understand

Translating job-relevant experiences from the unconventional and unusual into commercial language which employers understand and recognise, requires an understanding of current employment jargon and action verbs. 'Employer-ese' or business-credible language can be acquired through diligent reading of the business news and job vacancies, exploring a thesaurus and developing style alternatives. As Frances Bastress says: 'Unless you want to continue being a volunteer, avoid sounding like a volunteer'.

Many job-search publications suggest the use of action verbs in CVs and résumés. These are considered to be essential to a convincing CV, and help avoid repetitive and dull 'I' phrases ('I was/did/can/had'). They are also very economical as you do not use up valuable space or have to worry about elegant English. You will find a short list of action terms in Chapter 2, Information About Yourself (page 27) where additional reading is also suggested.

Some dos and don'ts for all CVs and résumés
Do

- stress the benefits of employing you
- relate your experience to the job

- convey your enthusiasm for the organisation
- demonstrate your abilities positively
- highlight what you can do
- begin sentences with *action* verbs, simple language
- ask yourself: 'will this piece of information help get the job?'
- sign and date application forms
- take copies of all applications

Do not

- include lengthy job descriptions, personal opinions
- include educational dates and course contents more than 15 years old
- include referees' details unless specifically required or without asking them first
- use unnecessary phrases, words such as 'volunteer' and 'part-time'
- use 'I'

Additionally, a CV or résumé is *not* intended to

- be a detailed history of all aspects of your life
- offer a complex record of every certificate you've ever gained
- present a soapbox for fascinating views on the world's problems
- be an exercise in English literature/grammar
- be heavy with technical jargon
- be an exaggeration or an under valuation
- be boring or vague
- be illegible, grubby or dirty
- cover more than one or two A4 pages
- get you a job – *repeat* – it is *not* meant to get you a job

Other written self-marketing material

Letters
Written communication in the form of job search, referral, cover or thank-you letters are particularly useful devices when searching for a job and self-marketing in a new location. You can use any

or all of the following to overview employment generally or for a specific job.

Job search or approach letters are written to ask for general information; they are 'fishing trips' or job prospecting efforts to contacts or strangers, and invite suggestions from them about the new area or for other people and networks to approach. These letters are short and to the point, but never beg or plead for work. Ask for advice of course, attach a brief CV and remember to follow up with a thank-you letter afterwards.

Referral letters are the next step up from job search leads and contacts. Again, you do not ask for work but invite an information interview as suggested in Chapter 3. This kind of letter should be simple and straightforward. Mention a mutual contact and include a CV, if you wish, although you may prefer to keep this for a face-to-face meeting. End the letter by saying what you will do next: telephone in one week's time, visit or suggest a drink together. A thank-you letter is appropriate after any meeting or advice.

Accompanying or cover letters are quite commonplace, especially in the USA and Australia. In many other countries, including the European Community, there are no set rules, so a businesslike, short and interesting letter is unlikely to disadvantage you. *Cover* letters accompany your CV or résumé; they highlight your special skills and qualities, explain omissions from application forms, show how your experience meets employer needs and they increase the impact of your personal contribution to an organisation.

These letters must be kept short; one page with three or four paragraphs only. Use clear, concise language and avoid spelling errors. If you speak a foreign employer's language fluently, certainly illustrate your skill, but only – repeat, *only* – if you are accurate.

Whenever possible, write to an individual. Find out the name and title of the person you wish to address from the telephone switchboard, company reports, advertisements, etc. Always keep a copy of your letter for future reference. What should be included in a cover letter? First of all, state why you are writing and mention any recent and relevant publicity about the firm. Next, present positive information about yourself which will be valuable to the company and include any clarification about CV or application form matters. Conclude by indicating how much you are looking forward to the opportunity to meet.

Thank-you letters (see page 99) are written after interviews or job offers and following assistance from contacts or referrals. They are not produced merely out of politeness. A thank-you letter reminds the receiver of your existence as well as giving you the opportunity to repeat something important about yourself or mention something you forgot to say at the time. You can also send a thank-you letter if you are rejected for a job. When you are particularly keen on an employer or work field, even though you did not get the job this time, you may like to use a letter to thank the interviewer for the time and effort, say what you have learned from the experience, ask for feedback and mention you will be glad to be considered for the next vacancy.

Interview skills for the highly mobile

The interview is the single most important step in obtaining a job offer. Whether you are seeking a domestic or an international job, everything you have done so far in your search for work is intended to gain a few minutes of face-to-face communication with a prospective employer. But, most people loathe interviews. It feels like a step into the unknown and there seem to be few ways of knowing in advance what you will be asked and whether your answers will help you to score over other candidates.

In general, it helps to realise that not all employers hold proficiency certificates in interviewing skills. Many are, frankly, amateurish, with only a vague idea of the sort of person they want to engage and an even woollier notion of how to find them. They may even hate the interviewing process as much or more than the applicant. Even if they do adopt a so-called 'scientific' screening process, interviewers may still resort to subjective opinions and first impressions in order to pick the person for the job.

A helpful idea, for you – the applicant – to bear in mind, is to regard the interview as an elimination process: the employer has, say, a dozen candidates whose written material more or less fits the requirements. From this group of 'possibles' will come one employee whose skills and experience will solve the vacancy problem – the one who will cause the employer *the minimum amount of trouble.* In the employer's eyes, *trouble* may be caused by children, elderly relatives, high-flying husbands/wives, international spouses, returners, ex-military, long-term unemployed, over 50s and so on – depending on personal prejudice and/or experience.

Your task, as a job-seeker on the move, is to convince the employer you are *not* going to be trouble – and you should aim to do so *within the first five minutes of the interview.* These vital first impressions may make or break your chances of success. How can you achieve this? Again, this section is not a thorough guide to all interviews; the following tips aim to help you over some of the hurdles and give you a chance to do your best at the interview.

Basic dos and don'ts for all interviews

- Plan your timetable and route to the interview venue. Aim to arrive 10 minutes early and be pleasant from the moment you come through the door, as secretaries and receptionists may also be involved in the selection process.
- Most interviews include typical general questions about your education, work experience and future goals. Refresh your memory from your application form, CV or résumé and prepare positive answers to fill in the gaps.
- Read about the company or organisation to help in answering the 'Why do you want to work for us?' question. Consult company reports, directories, business section of national newspapers, other workers. If necessary, ask for help at your reference library. (Note: Some UK areas have video data Company Reports. Ask at your local Careers Office.)
- First impressions count. Dress smartly. Don't bring along plastic bags of shopping, pets, snacks, cigarettes. Be aware of your body language: smile, use appropriate eye contact and an alert posture. Memorise and address the interviewer(s) by name(s).
- Don't giggle, wriggle or wag your fingers. Avoid monologues:

keep the interviewer's attention – they may be bored and if you send them to sleep, you've failed!

- Don't interrupt, shout or complain. Don't try to control the interview: you probably need them more than they need you!
- Never, *never*, belittle a former boss, colleagues or company. Instead, give an unbiased reason why you left the last job. At the same time, do not criticise your partner, family, the government or society.
- Have ready some questions of your own (see below). Clarify exactly what the job involves, under and with whom you will be working, the working environment, benefits and restrictions. Always ask when you can expect to hear about a decision.

Questions portable career seekers may expect to be asked
'Why are you applying for a job so far from home?'
'Why do you want to live in . . . ?'
'Why do you want a career change now?'
'How long do you expect to stay in . . . ?'
'What kind of work does your husband/wife do?'
'How do you explain all the different kinds of job you've had?'
'Why have you stayed so long with the same company?'
'How long have you been out of work now?'
'What do you think will be the main difficulties in fitting into civilian life?'
'Do you drink/smoke? How is your stamina?'
'How well could you work under a younger boss?'
'Are you not over-qualified for this job?'
'How will you cope with the climate (or food, culture, language or loneliness)?'
'What other countries have you worked in?'
'How soon can you move?'
'Have you worked with foreign/civilian/rural/ . . . staff before?'

Note. International job-seekers should expect to be asked cross-cultural and personal questions in addition to ones on work content and technical proficiency. *All interviews in a new location* may include questions about your ability to fit into the new surroundings.

International career seekers should ask about

- Opportunities to meet former relocated employees
- Look-see visits prior to contract
- Exact dates and duration of employment
- Comprehensive details of job (teachers: look carefully at contract hours)
- Employment contract terms: renewal, termination, penalties
- Salary package: currency, tax liabilities, allowances, bonuses, benefits
- Immigration matters, work permits, visas
- Packing and shipping of personal goods abroad and on re-entry
- Accommodation, temporary and permanent, home and abroad
- Transport: local and international
- Arrangements for children
- Domestic help, cost of living
- Medical and social facilities, local lifestyle, other expatriates
- Political climate, safety and security
- Spouse employment locally
- Local voluntary organisations
- Local adult educational facilities
- Holiday visits by children, older relatives
- Provision for pets
- Home leave

Afterwards

Many prospective employers appreciate a short letter after the interview. Thank the interviewer for the time and opportunity to meet and mention any aspects of the interview you wish to clarify or highlight. Close on a positive note: say how much you look forward to joining the company, contributing to their project, keeping in touch. Enclose any relevant documentation or contact details for referees. American employers expect you to market yourself confidently; British recruiters may be more sceptical, so word your note of thanks accordingly.

If you did not remember to ask at the interview when a decision will be made about the job, telephone to enquire. Simply ask for the interviewer's secretary, state your name, the job applied for and the interview date. Is it worth telephoning to find out why you did not get the job? Yes, it is always worth a try, provided you remain polite and unruffled and do not expect elaborate feedback. All interviews have value, even those at which you are rejected. It is good experience and one from which you can learn. Ask yourself: how can you do better next time? Which questions caused you difficulty? How can you reply more convincingly? And then, move on with your job search.

6. Settling In

This chapter looks at some of the stages you may experience when adapting to a strange place and contains ideas for developing a personal support system, fitting in with new work colleagues and, lastly, suggestions for families, dual-career couples and singles. As Natasha Josefowitz observes: 'The road from outside to insider may be rocky, but it has identifiable steps. Knowing the pitfalls will not make them disappear, but it will make the crossing easier.'

The settling-in process

Talk to anyone who has just moved all their belongings from one place to another and they will probably groan 'Never, never again!' Yet for many families, moving is a way of life. Military personnel, diplomatic officials, oil and mining employees regularly transfer to new locations, sometimes after just a few months and with little forewarning. If you are facing a first relocation, it is comforting to know in advance how you may react to the change and be reassured that your experiences are part of a longer-term adjustment process. Adaptation to living in a new place has several stages of which, for simplicity, the three main ones are described here: contact, disintegration and reintegration.

The upheaval associated with packing up one's home, travelling to a strange place and then sorting everything out again is overwhelming but exhilarating. Whether you welcomed or objected to relocation, the physical activity makes you feel excited and keeps you too busy to feel anything apart from just plain tired. You have a sense of relief: relief that the waiting and uncertainty is over and the upheaval has finished. At long last, you say to yourself, I can now get on with my life. It is a heady, fascinating feeling. You are curious, interested and happy, just like the first cheerful days of a holiday. This is the first stage of the adaptation cycle, the *contact* phase, a time of initial euphoria lasting for about a month.

As the honeymoon wanes, a sense of reality creeps in and the new surroundings lose their appeal. This second stage, called *disintegration*, is when less pleasant feelings are likely to surface: a sense of loss, feeling unwanted, disliking everything and everybody, loneliness, resentment, depression. Disintegration may be specially marked if you have moved to another country, with a different culture and language, when you cannot make yourself understood or know how or where to go. If there are travel restrictions, electricity cuts, water shortages, security worries, foreign staff and above all, no close friends to talk to, you may become particularly stressed. Culture shock, the stress caused by a sudden change of location, is very unpleasant: you feel acutely stressed, homesick, rejected, angry, withdrawn and frustrated.

Eventually – sometimes after many months – the new surroundings become more familiar and all the differences start to disappear. Perhaps you have learned to speak a few phrases in the new language and begun to find your way around; you know, now, how to post a letter, where the bus stops, what food to purchase. Life becomes more predictable, relaxed and familiar. As you gradually settle more and more into the host location, the *reintegration* phase begins. Soon, you are no longer a newcomer, this is 'home' for you now; and as you participate increasingly in the new community and successfully adapt to the new environment, settling in becomes complete.

Of course, not everyone reacts to relocation in the same way. Some individuals settle in very quickly, suffering few if any obviously distressing symptoms of culture shock. Others feel as if they have become 'stuck' in the disintegration stage forever and will never settle in. It is certainly uncommon not to experience *some* degree of emotional discomfort in a new posting; the most likely pattern is to move fitfully back and forth from one adaptation stage to another.

To counteract some of the unpleasant settling-in stages, both the employee and the transferring partner need to develop a range of flexible coping skills. There are some positive ideas in the following sections.

Emotional reactions to relocation

Even when there is no language difference, in, for example, a domestic relocation, settling in takes time. A sensible and realistic plan is to allow yourself a good interval to adjust to your changed circumstances. Expect life to be less than rosy immediately following the move and for a while after that.

Adjustment reactions are more likely to show up on overseas transfers, where every aspect of living is entirely new, but difficulties can also occur nearer home. Going from north to south Britain, countryside to city, suburbia to isolated farmland, let alone across continents, climates and cultures evokes some, or all of the following reactions: shock and panic, feeling numb and frozen, disbelief and denial, anger and irritability, guilt and depression. Physical symptoms may occur: headaches, lassitude, rashes. To cope, it may be all too easy to take just one more drink – or cigarette, or tranquilliser – or to overeat, diet too much or exhibit another of the 'comfort' types of behaviour we all fall back upon in times of stress.

The most important point to make here is this: even when we expect joyful and pleasurable new experiences (winning the pools, marriage, the first baby) our behaviour goes through a series of emotional changes and stages. It is not wrong, bad or un-British to feel strong emotions; what is unhealthy and unwise is to pretend they do not exist.

Culture shock is increased and the settling-in process takes longer when individuals are plunged into an extremely different environment from the one they are accustomed to, especially when differences in values and social behaviour are very marked. As with many other aspects of relocation, thorough pre-departure information about the new location and its lifestyle aids successful adaptation. Learning the language – just basic, simple, everyday phrases – makes life easier, as does finding contacts and colleagues who are willing to act as short-term guides and mentors. Link into company contacts, spouse/partner groups, sports clubs, welcoming circles and relocation personnel. Ongoing contact with home-based professional networks, college associations, social, leisure and community groups decreases the sense of isolation during the early stages. Keep writing and telephoning the family and friends back home. Talk things out, be assertive, write it out and laugh at life whenever possible!

It has been suggested that relocation is similar to bereavement, and for anyone experiencing acute difficulties in coming to terms with the change, personal counselling is advisable. Contact the British Association for Counselling for *accredited* counsellors who help individuals learn new ways of coping with loss. Relevant books include those concerned with managing stress; alternative therapies, especially those concerned with relaxation and good posture (eg Alexander Technique and yoga), are also useful.

Relationships

The settling-in process puts heavy demands on relationships. Couples anticipate support from each other during the adaptation process but when one partner becomes thoroughly absorbed in the new life while the other has not yet made friends, found a job or niche of their own, relationships are prone to suffer. The non-working spouse, having no one to talk to, no confidante and no close friendships, becomes rejected, jealous, frustrated and angry. Strains between the pair, previously unnoticed, tend to come to the surface and pressure the settling-in process even more. Marriage difficulties, which are not unknown in expatriate circles, could follow.

Wendy Coyle, writing about moving in Australia, suggests that families should plan to be 'closed' for a while following relocation and away-from-home travel limited to allow each partner time, affection and attention for each other. Other researchers suggest it is important to return to a familiar routine as soon as possible, with shared mealtimes and joint recreational activities. Above all, an awareness of each other's feelings and quality talking time reduces the stress upon relationships. If post-move counselling is offered during the adjustment process, couples who find themselves under severe tension should take up such opportunities.

The old style 'trailing spouse' is no longer necessarily female. Trailing husbands must ask themselves in advance: to what extent are they willing (and able) to take on the settling-in tasks normally accomplished by women? How will they fit into the predominantly female daytime round of coffee mornings, tennis and charity groups? How will they cope with loneliness, isolation, rejection and loss? And what will be their own career future should this relocation be the first of many? During the planning period prior to transfer, all couples, regardless of employment, should discuss relationship matters together very thoroughly.

Developing a new personal support system

Perhaps the greatest difficulties occur when your personal support system is far away. Human beings are social animals and a personal support system consists of those close friends who you really know and who know you well – trustworthy, special people in your life to whom you can talk freely about absolutely anything. Mum around the corner, soul mates who are always 'there' when things go wrong, kindred spirits and close comrades – these are the people most missed and hardest to replace when you move. It takes time and care to establish a new personal support system. Highly mobile families, those forced to move away for long periods or at very frequent intervals, face special problems; opportunities to keep up home-based friendships tend to dilute, fragment and then disappear, leaving lonely voids impossible to fill.

How do you set about finding a new personal support system away from home? If you have not done your homework about facilities in the new location before the move, do so now or as soon as possible. For *overseas* assignments, especially in the USA, find out if there is an established welcome group for newcomers and what it has to offer. Read travel guides about the local lifestyle, ask relocation personnel, orientation programmes, briefing and resource courses about expatriate facilities. Within Britain, information on local groups and activities is usually available from libraries, town halls, tourist boards, volunteer and Citizens' Advice Bureaux.

Children are said to be the fastest route into a new community in any country, with pets (especially dogs) coming a close second within the UK. Personal introductions are invaluable, so make sure to spread the word before you leave home. Take the names, addresses and telephone numbers of anyone known to your family, friends and colleagues – and *contact them*. It does not matter, at first, whether these people are compatible with you or not: use the link as a starting point. Be friendly to everyone while you find your feet and begin to build bridges.

Other sources of contacts and groups include:

- Priest, minister or rabbi
- Sports clubs
- Baby clinic, play group, nursery
- Rotary/British Legion; other veterans' groups
- Academic departments, societies
- Women's and men's groups/networks
- Professional associations
- Charities and their field workers

'It is important not to "jump in" to . . . friendship', writes Wendy Coyle. 'You should "test the water" first – be conscious of your friend's response to your confidences and don't "pour your heart out" too soon . . . try to become close gradually – it avoids embarrassment if the other person does not yet want this depth of friendship.' Families, particularly husbands, should fill the void while you gradually build up new friends to confide in over several months, but take note of the possible relationship strains mentioned above.

The 'art of conversation' sounds a very out-dated concept, but it is a valuable social talent at which some expatriate spouses seem to excel. Probably they have had more practice than most of us when they relocate and start up new friendships over and over again. If you are lacking confidence in communication skills, feel

Table 6.1 *Personal network inventory*

	Home	Now
Family		
Close friends contemporaries other age groups		
Acquaintances		
Spiritual support (church, synagogue, etc)		
Intellectual circle		
Work colleagues		
Team mates (sports, hobbies)		
Professionals (doctor, lawyer, etc)		
Animals (comfort, exercise)		
Others		

shy about making the first move or missed out on learning the 'rules' of small talk, take an assertiveness, social interaction, public speaking or effective presentation course. *Talk Small*, by Peter Daly is a useful guide to body language and conversation in business and social occasions.

Another useful idea is to take a 'personal network inventory' as a reference base. List your home support system, by name or initials as you prefer, under the categories suggested (add more if necessary) and then use it for developing companions in the new location (see Table 6.1).

Maintaining home contacts

You will want to keep in touch with contacts from home even after you have moved away. During the settling-in process and for some time afterwards, letters and telephone calls from family and good friends can make all the difference to your well being. Apart from practical problems (furniture storage, school holidays, tenants, pets, garden, etc) which you need to manage from a distance, keeping in touch with home bridges the gap between old and new personal support systems.

These are the people to help you over the stressful times, the disintegration period. Use your personal network inventory to identify key individuals who will be willing and able to listen to or read about your feelings and experiences. Prepare them in advance, if necessary; explain that you will not necessarily require advice or practical assistance but will value their role as your special confidants to help you through the adaptation process.

There are other reasons for keeping in touch. If, eventually, you expect to return home, you will want to take up family, friends, neighbours, community and work contacts once more. Life at home will change and move on while you are away. It is no use expecting everyone to be really thrilled to see you again unless you have made some effort to keep in touch with their lives, too. So, write letters, record cassettes, send Christmas and birthday cards, read the newspapers, ask for photographs, have the local papers sent on, listen to the BBC World Service (Voice of America, Radio Australia), exchange videos.

Settling in with work colleagues

So, you've arrived in town, unpacked the boxes and bags, had a quick look around the district and now it is Monday morning, time for work. How do you, the new employee, settle into the new job? Just like the general transition, settling in at work has distinct stages: the *honeymoon period* when you are too busy to notice anything wrong; *disintegration*, when nothing seems right and, eventually, *reintegration* and independence.

It makes sense not to expect too much of yourself or work colleagues during the early days. Josefowitz and Gadon suggest four aspects to adapting in the new work situation: firstly, expect your level of performance to be low at first. Do not blame yourself if you are not as efficient as before, for, even after several months in the new job, you may underperform by as much as half compared to previously. Then, expect to be exhausted and expect to be stressed. The value of home contacts and familiar routine is again highlighted as they help you to feel so much more at home. Make use now of stress management techniques, especially relaxation. Finally, expect a letdown when you least expect it – the disintegration stage may come upon you quite suddenly and last for longer than you anticipate. As Josefowitz and Gadon say, 'Be patient with yourself'.

Try to keep a low profile with colleagues at first while you discover who is where and what is the office pecking order and their cliques, jokes, rituals and hidden agendas. Don't talk about your last boss, salary, personal matters, but make as many non-committed contacts as possible. And, above all, smile and listen a lot!

Families

As a small child during World War II, I went to ten different schools. I travelled up and down England and Wales with a middle-aged spinster aunt, spending a few months here, half a year there. I even made several visits to the same place, but rarely attended the same school more than once. In the long run, my academic education and social development suffered considerably as I never knew which book or topic to expect from lessons and I found it impossible to make friends when I was never anywhere long enough to get to know anyone properly. Nevertheless, I made one important discovery, something of life-long value: I found out how to discover the route to the nearest loos in record time – an extremely practical transferable lifeskill!

Research on relocation clearly indicates that my experience was not unique. Parents worry about the education and social behaviour of their children, especially the teenagers. Although not one expert has yet decided whether or not relocation has bad effects on children, it makes sense to prepare them for the move as early as possible; encourage them to talk about how they feel, what differences to expect, how to cope with the change. For educational guidance on relocation, specialist advice may be necessary.

Even the smallest children can be supported by helping them to keep in touch with family and home-based friends. Postcards and photographs can be sent to and from grandparents, cousins, playmates, school friends; cassettes and videos to and from 'home' are also comforting. Settling-in time should be adjusted to each child's need, with as swift a return to a regular family routine as possible. Favourite meals, activities, toys, games and gadgets (pets, too, within Britain), all help to maintain some semblance of stability in what is, often, an exciting but confusing experience for the young.

Dual-career couples

Time and energy are pressured during the settling-in period for both partners. Their mutual support system may be under considerable strain so time management strategies and relationship communication are essential. Talk together about the possible problems and worries, recognise life is going to be stressed and plan together-time – going out for a meal, doing-nothing periods, sufficient holidays, even a soothing bath time – as seriously as if it were a business appointment. Buy together-time by using the best paid help and domestic support services available. But, above all, learn to relax, have fun, share life and laugh together.

Singles

All transferees are short of time when they move: time for the practical aspects of relocation, time for settling in, time for the emotional adjustment to the new life. But for singles – male or female – on assignments away from home, settling in is particularly complex. They have only one pair of hands to house hunt, unpack and arrange a home while simultaneously coping with the new workplace and unfamiliar colleagues. Leaving loved ones makes life more difficult; starting up a social life from scratch adds to their problems.

Rumour has it that resident expatriate wives make matters far worse for single businesswomen abroad because so-called 'help-less' bachelors are eagerly supported and cared for by the host community, while incoming unattached females are completely ignored. Helpful ideas for solo women transferees include finding accommodation among other singles, creating social opportunities by inviting in the neighbours, getting to know one or two families really well, polishing your social skills, taking up bridge and/or a sport. Dating is a problem for single women; they are less likely to belong to local clubs or associations and local cultural customs may preclude many activities if they travel unaccompanied. Look to local interest groups – music, art, museums, theatre, university, religious and so on – for opportunities to meet other unattached persons. When I was a teenager, my father always insisted that I had enough emergency money on me to come home by taxi. I believe this remains good advice for women, of any age, at social events world-wide.

If you are a single female and about to be transferred to a foreign location, find out in advance about suitable residential areas, no-go areas and appropriate dress and behaviour. You will need to be very well organised (which you probably are already, otherwise your firm would not be relocating you!) because you are the only person who will be taking care of you. Plan in advance important aspects of the move such as medical cover, time off, back-up help, automobile availability and telephone installation (both are essential for solo women), safe car parking, good street lighting, nearby neighbours. Discuss the possibility of taking a relative along with you, for the short-term at least, someone who can deal with the domestic arrangements while you are at the office. This may be more practical for domestic relocations, but is also worth considering for moves further afield.

Dealing with new workplace colleagues may present special challenges for the relocated female. If she is also the first woman transferee in that organisation, her task may be particularly challenging. Research has pointed out that other colleagues, rather than cultural differences, are likely to make life difficult for transferred women. Try not to resort to 'iron lady' tactics; by all means stay businesslike, but maintain an amicable and friendly style. As opposed to personal friendships, your relationships with men at work should be professional, appropriate to your position and level of authority. One-to-one social relationships with male colleagues should be firmly avoided until you are well settled in. On the other hand, invitations from families and women co-workers are welcome starting points.

7. What Can You Do If You Cannot Work in Your Chosen Field?

Overseas employment restrictions

Most countries exercise control over the employment of foreigners. Alien work permits are frequently limited to workers in certain job categories and become available only after the employer has tried to fill the position from the resident labour market. Wives and husbands of employees may or may not receive a work permit, depending on the regulations of individual countries. Unmarried partners are rarely, if ever, allowed to work unless they apply in their own right. Details about work permits are constantly changing, so it makes sense to find out about them from the relevant embassy or consulate well in advance.

An overseas transfer involves much paperwork: always assume that employment restrictions, visas, work permits, vaccination certificates, medical fitness evidence and similar are required unless you are definitely informed otherwise. Find out if your UK qualifications are valid and recognised. Make early contact with the appropriate officials for the most up-to-date details. Some experts advise prospective employees to double check information as incorrect or misunderstood information may be given out inadvertently; ask twice as a useful back-up measure. If you have a job already arranged, your future employer may apply for a work permit – and pay for it – and then send it on to you. This is not automatic, however, so make sure you check.

Do not simply *expect* spouse employment will be permitted in your new location. It is essential to find out exactly what paid work accompanying married partners may or may not undertake in the transfer country prior to departure from the UK. Even if you have not the slightest desire to work now, it is always possible that your mind or circumstances could change and, quite unwittingly, you could transgress some local regulation. Do your homework early on to avoid difficulties later.

When you cannot work

If you are unable to take up any paid employment whatsoever in the new location, it is all too easy to drift into a structureless void. Instead, plan to use the time fruitfully. If you have completed the self-assessment exercises in Chapter 2 or taken professional career/life planning guidance, you will already have some action plans and set goals. For example, you may have made a positive, informed decision to spend your time away from home acquiring fresh job-relevant skills, through unpaid posts or further education and training. Your task then is to research as many possible openings for yourself in order to achieve your goal.

When paid employment is impossible, your choices include:

- taking time out for personal development
- having a family break
- non-paid work
- education and training
- studying abroad and internship programmes

1. Taking time out for personal development

As a small child, I was in a hurry to be grown-up. I firmly believed adults knew everything and were thoroughly competent at absolutely anything. How wrong I was! It has taken most of my adult years to begin to understand just a few of the answers and learn how to get through some quite ordinary events. I would have welcomed some 'time out', though, away from the hurly-burly of everyday life, to evaluate and improve my self-management and relationship skills. If you choose to take time out for personal development, a selection of skills to consider is offered below.

Self-management skills, sometimes known as 'I' skills, are needed to manage our lives and to grow as people. They include basic literacy and numeracy, learning how to solve problems, manage time, discover values and beliefs, make decisions, cope with stress, keep fit, find information and resources.

Relationships are the core of our lives and their success or failure provides us with happiness or misery or, more probably, a mixture of both. *Human relationship*, or 'Me and You', skills include effective interpersonal communication, assertiveness, good listening, managing conflict and change, group participation, intimacy and the expression of feelings.

For some, there are personal development skills related to specific situations: understanding finance, legal and consumer rights, resisting persuasion, car maintenance, basic household repairs, public speaking, asking for help, survival skills such as self-defence, life saving, and first aid. Consider, also, social skills: overcoming shyness, conversational skills, body language, interactive sports and other pastimes such as bridge, golf and chess.

2. A family break

When I stopped work as an accompanist to have my first child, I planned to return to work as soon as the baby was a few months old. How over-optimistic I was, how blissfully ignorant! Without child care, it was impossible to practise regularly and plain ridiculous to expect professional singers to compete with neonatal lung exercises. Twelve years later, when my youngest child climbed up the nursery school steps for the first time, I literally skipped all the way home. By then, though, there was no job to go back to: I was just another occupational invisible – another 'just a housewife'. My own solution was a complete change of direction and a new career.

Now I have few regrets about all the years I spent away from work. I had time to enjoy my children's infancy and early schooldays, and they had space and time to be with me. Young mothers now return to the workplace within months, not years, of giving birth, especially in managerial and professional occupations. They sometimes feel pressured to go back to the workplace by contemporaries or finance, and suffer guilt, divided loyalties and 'burnout' stress. I am not suggesting whether it is right or wrong for mothers to return to work after having a baby. Ideally, I believe all parents should, whenever possible, be allowed to choose whether or not they wish to be employed during the family's early years. Whenever a career break occurs, however, it impacts on personal, partner and professional life and is an irreversible decision.

If you find you are unable to work in the new location, you may decide to take a family break and spend time with youngsters or even older relatives. Once again, this should be a positive and informed decision, based upon good, fully assessed information.

3. Non-paid work

Many job-relevant skills can be acquired during a non-employed period by offering your services without pay. These are not always obvious qualifications, more a range of subtle accomplishments and transferable skills to enhance you – both as a person and as an employee. While you gain practical and enriched experience, you also demonstrate initiative, a positive attitude and establish community contacts (don't forget these are marketable qualities – include them in your CV). Share your competencies with others (and discover how to teach at the same time), discover a specialism, develop an unsung talent.

Some job-relevant skill suggestions

- Computer skills: database and spreadsheet management, word processing
- Financial skills: from simple bookkeeping to profit and loss accounts
- People skills: public speaking, negotiating, interviewing, trouble-shooting
- Group skills: committee collaboration, chairing meetings, delegation
- Writing skills, reports, minutes, presentations
- Marketing skills: advertising copy, public relations
- Selling skills
- Business social etiquette

- Recruitment skills: staff selection and interviewing, appraising, firing

Learn from volunteering, jobs in non-profit organisations, work in an 'observer' role. Ideally, you should look for a minimum of five job-related skills in non-paid work. At first, help out and take advantage of whatever exists in the new location, even if it means pouring out the tea – but keep an eye open for a step towards work-associated positions and upward mobility. In the long run, your aim should be to match the level of unpaid work with your employment plans.

It is important to keep full and accurate details of your non-paid activities for your career portfolio. Record exactly what you accomplished, how much you raised, how many you helped, which goals you achieve (and how). Ask the top person in the organisation for a reference, making sure it is written on headed paper and personally signed. Keep your records carefully in your career portfolio, alongside photocopies, for use in résumés, CVs and interviews.

To find non-paid work in UK location, contact the local volunteer bureau or rural community council; also ask the public library or town hall. Non-paid work overseas may be available through aid agency field workers or local groups in your relocation country. *Volunteer Work* is a directory of establishments recruiting volunteers world-wide and is available from the Central Bureau for Educational Visits and Exchanges, Seymour Mews House, Seymour Mews, London W1H 9PE. A useful introductory pack 'Thinking about Volunteering' is available from Returned Volunteer Action (RVA), 1 Amwell Street, London EC1R 1VL. A selection of voluntary organisations may be found in Useful Resources.

4. Education and training
If your qualifications, skills and experience do not seem to be suitable for transfer to anything or anywhere else, you may consider education and training as a new route into the world of work. A short- or longer-term course offers increased knowledge, contacts and up-to-date referees in the new field.

Choosing a course requires good information about your existing knowledge as well as the courses available. Try to link the study field to something about which you already have some experience, but, above all, go for a course which excites you. If, for instance, you think a business studies course will be boring but useful, think carefully before you enrol. It is hard enough to sustain motivation for even a fun part-time evening course during November and February; a longer study project is many times more difficult. Many colleges have open days or short 'taster' courses; take advantage of these to talk to department tutors or to find out if a subject is stimulating, before making a long commitment.

Aspiring mature students may hesitate to return to learning if it is many years since they studied textbooks, wrote essays and sat exams. They worry about entry requirements, concentrating for long periods and memorising facts and figures. These days most educational institutions welcome older learners on all courses. Useful general guidelines for prospective mature students, as set out by The Council for National Academic Awards (CNAA) suggest 'non-traditional entrants' should be able to provide reasonable evidence of their capacity to 'meet successfully the demands of the course for which they have applied'. The admission of individual students is usually at the discretion of the institution itself; some institutions require older candidates to undertake tests as well as interviews; others ask applicants to complete a suitable preparatory course. Always write for a detailed prospectus and make enquiries about different entry criteria.

It is often possible to visit institutions and arrange a discussion with a member of staff. This is a good time to find out about mature student entry requirements and see what life is like there as a student. Are there many mature students? Is study skill help available? Is the course examined, continually assessed, based on project work? Is there any career help?

To update your study skills, increase confidence and provide recent study evidence, consider taking GCSEs or A levels, or enrolling in an Access or Fresh Start programme. Also there are refresher courses at local adult education colleges. Study skill topics include efficient note-taking, essay writing, speed reading, time organisation and revision strategies for examinations.

For flexible educational opportunities that take account of prior learning or experience, the CNAA uses a Credit Accumulation and Transfer Scheme. CATS enables students to transfer from one course or institution to another during their studies. Details are available from ECCTIS 2000, a computerised service holding information on almost 80,000 courses in over 700 institutions throughout the UK. Other sources of information include PICKUP, a training directory and database intended to help people at work update their skills and the TAP database of training and educational opportunities. Information on both of these can be found at jobcentres, careers offices and various local authority Education Shops.

Sometimes, worries exist about course exits. Is it 'vocational? Will it lead directly into work? Will further training be necessary? There are few, if any, guaranteed pathways from education into employment at any age; for adult, mature learners difficulties sometimes occur in persuading employers they have the relevant experience (not just qualifications) to fill the vacancy. One answer is to use your studies to increase your contacts and network opportunities. Student life is not just reading lists and exams. It is college social activities, workshops, debates, seminars, conferences, clubs and societies. Increase your visibility and talk to everyone (tutors as well as fellow students) so that you become known and know others for post-educational opportunities.

The most comprehensive national guide to adult education and training opportunities in Britain is *Second Chances* available in libraries or from book shops, some careers offices or direct from Careers and Occupational Information Centre (COIC), Moorfoot, Sheffield S1 4PQ. Also the *Kogan Page Mature Student's Handbook* (see Useful Resources).

The National Council for Vocational Qualifications (NCVQ) brings together standards of competence. Information from NCVQ, 222 Euston Road, London NW1 3BZ.

To check UK equivalents of foreign qualifications attained at overseas academic institutions, community colleges, international schools and colleges, etc, contact The National Academic Recognition Information Centre (NARIC) for the United Kingdom, British Council, Medlock Street, Manchester M15 4PR; (061-957 7000).

Independent colleges. The British Accreditation Council for Independent Further and Higher Education inspects and accredits private institutions. BAC, 114 Chase Side, Southgate, London N14 5PH.

National Extension College. Distance learning material is available everywhere but it may depend on what course you wish to take and the country in which you want to learn. For example, you are unlikely to have facilities to study advanced electronics in an African village. Postage may add to costs and mail delivery problems should be taken into account. The best advice is to keep copies of everything posted (so you will need access to a photocopier). The National Extension College encourages prospective students to make full enquiries by telephoning or writing to: National Extension College, 18 Brooklands Avenue, Cambridge CB2 2HN.

The Open University. Enquiries are welcome for overseas distance learning courses although availability may depend on subject and location. Contact the Cambridge Regional Centre (0223 64721) and ask for 'Euroclerk'.

Studying abroad and internship programmes
There are academic opportunities for adults in countries outside Britain and often these offer a speedy route into the international community and employment contacts. You should evaluate the courses before enrolling: How much are the fees and who will pay them? Is the institution accredited by a recognised authority? In what language are courses taught? Is the course recognised at home? Does the programme fit into your portable career goals?

Your first step towards learning abroad should be to contact the Embassy or High Commission of the country. Most are located in London and will inform you about study opportunities and rules for students. You should be able to study in all the European Community countries without difficulty. To find out what is available, first ask at your local jobcentre, careers office or ask your local authority if it has set up a European information and advice centre. If not, contact the Department of Education and Science (081-952 2366) for recent publications. *Second Chances* (see above and Useful Resources section) has a section on 'Learners Abroad'.

American and Canadian institutions have less rigid course structures but note that *all* are fee paying, even the state universities. Application procedures vary so much you must approach individual colleges for further information. In general, prospective students (undergraduate and postgraduate) must take standardised aptitude tests as an essential part of the application procedure. If you wish to apply to a business school, you must take the Graduate Management Admissions Test (GMAT). The US/UK Educational Commission and the Fulbright Commission are valuable sources of detailed information. Also useful: The Association of Commonwealth Universities, the Central Bureau and UNESCO (publications available from HMSO).

Internships
Internships are on-the-job training opportunities or work experience packages. They are offered mainly to graduates wishing to gain experience in organisations or at colleges but may also be available to adult career changers and returners. Some internships are part time while others range from six months to a year or so on a full-time basis. Usually these opportunities are without pay, although some employers may offer a small stipend. Internships may lead to a job offer or you could find the experience useful for networking and contacts. Foreign applicants for US internships require a proper visa before entering the United States. A sponsor is required to arrange the necessary paperwork.

To apply for an internship in the United States, you must prepare a résumé that includes an internship objective (related to the position applied for), your educational details and related experience. References will be required. Send a covering letter (see Chapter 5). If you attend an interview, learn as much about the company as possible beforehand. It is usual to have a signed agreement between you and your internship sponsor covering your basic responsibilities and objectives.

Look out for *Internships 1992* (annual publication) published by Peterson's Guides, Princeton, New Jersey, USA, available at British bookshops and libraries. Internships are also listed in the current edition of Bolles' *What Color Is your Parachute?*.

If you can work, but not in your chosen field

If you can work but, however hard you try, you cannot find any opportunities in your own field, consider adding a new dimension to your employment portfolio. Opportunities may exist to acquire local, specialist skills and consolidate undeveloped ones. Become an expert on your new home area and pack that enterprise into your bags for the next move. Once again, your completed self-assessment exercises will be helpful in identifying appropriate and potentially rewarding aspects. Some suggestions for overseas and domestic assignments follow.

Overseas examples
- local ethnic expertise
- language skills
- local professional competencies
- international corporate practices
- foreign currency knowledge
- foreign exchange know-how
- local communication/marketing
- local economic trends, sales techniques

Domestic suggestions
- local business networks
- office politics
- small town/big city culture
- regional craft expertise
- local population trends
- social/gender/age differences

Self-employment and freelance work

The most portable and flexible option open to anyone on the move is self-employment. Self-employment offers many advantages: it is a challenge, you use existing expertise, retain independence, gain variety and may even make a little money. But there are disadvantages too: many small businesses fail because of insufficient capital, the hours are long, profits are more likely to be losses, interruptions, isolation and overwork are commonplace.

Starting your own business requires more than just a good idea and enthusiasm as there are several stages to cover before your business gets off the ground. These include: choosing an idea that interests you and builds on existing skills (manufacturing, wholesaling, retailing or a service); obtaining further training if necessary; working out how much to charge; making a business plan; finding premises, equipment, suppliers etc; marketing your business; and recording transactions. The range of financial skills required includes bookkeeping, budget control, understanding tax, VAT and National Insurance, sales and stock management, overheads . . . the list is endless.

Publicity and advertising methods depend on the type of business you intend to run. You will need graphic design help for some of the following publicity material: printed catalogues, leaflets, business cards, letterheads, posters. The cheapest (and arguably best) form of advertising is 'word of mouth' recommendation, but it can be very slow to build up a business this way. Consider local and national newspapers, trade magazines, trade fairs, craft shows, exhibitions, Yellow Pages, Thomson Guides, press releases to local media, shop windows and local notice boards. However, be sure you have the capacity to handle a large response since failure to fill or complete a contract may mean business is lost forever.

Research regulations before starting your own business and pay special attention to local licensing laws and neighbourhood restrictions. If you intend working from home and your occupation is reasonably quiet, you are unlikely to require planning permission, but if there is a constant stream of visitors or goods deliveries, noisy machinery or nasty smells your neighbours may well object. Check with your local town hall first. Also, consult your household insurance company for any special prerequisites. Food prepared in the home is subject to strict health conditions and regulations. Contact the local Inspector through the Town Hall. If you care for other people's children in your home as a child minder, it is necessary to be registered.

If you relocate often, consider the ease (or difficulty) of transferring your business with each move. For those seriously interested in freelancing or setting up a business, an excellent investment is to enrol in one of the many small business courses available nation-wide. Consult the current edition of *Second Chances* for details of training for self-employment.

Working freelance is attractive to portable career seekers. As a freelance, you can teach, offer a service, set up as an independent, become a sole practitioner or call yourself 'Consultant' in practically anything. It is a more transferable form of self-employment requiring little heavy equipment, few overheads and small start-up costs. Photography, writing, craft work, restoration, repairing, catering, art and design are some of the freelance services easy to transport to a new location. Think about continuity of work: not only must you be proficient at the service to be offered, but you must also maintain your visibility and self-marketing in order to keep a flow of work coming in.

You may decide to offer your professional business services, skills to companies or individual clients on short-term contract or consultancy basis. Here you gain some level of security and income. Employers vary in their attitude to consultants. Some engage specialist services readily as a cost-efficient use of resources; others remain unconvinced. A freelance person with convincing, excellent credentials is more likely to gain contracts than an amateurish, unsure approach. Take a course, talk to others in the field and read about it first.

If you are relocating overseas, you are advised to check before departure whether there are any local restrictions on freelance or self-employed work.

Telecommuting/teleworking

Telecommuting arrangements usually involve employees spending some part of their time working at a computer away from the office. This may be a home-based location, or from a satellite office or work centre. You may be able to explore the telecommuting option with your present employer or negotiate assignments with a new firm. Several points are worth noting: telecommuting is *not* the answer to child care problems so first ensure that appropriate help is available and you are as free from interruptions as possible. Domestic circumstances must be suitable for productive work and your residence secure enough to protect all equipment. Some workers feel isolated without their colleagues and they must ensure that they are temperamentally and emotionally suited to working away from an office environment. On the practical side, efficient power sources are essential, as are technical and servicing facilities. While, at the moment, this is an innovative arrangement, teleworking is certainly worth exploring. In the future, as a recent researcher pointed out, teleworking may provide a means for spouses to accept overseas posting of their partners more easily.

Flexible patterns of work

The International Society of Work Options, based in the USA, is concerned with innovative working arrangements and its members, including researchers and practitioners, promote and explore non-traditional work schedules. One American member provides 'Good-bye 9–5!' presentations; others offer seminars, training programmes and policy initiatives on imaginative work/time options.

Flexible patterns of work are becoming more commonplace in many countries. One London local authority offers job-share opportunities and flexitime to baby-break returners; another employer will negotiate annual hours programmes for the parents of schoolchildren. All these and similar arrangements have relevance to portable careers.

An annual hours concept involves an employee agreeing to

work a negotiated number of hours during the year but the time when these hours may be worked is flexible, within agreed limits. A good example of this is when a spouse works full- or overtime during children's term-time, but only part-time hours during school holidays.

Part-time work is of course, well known, as is *job-sharing*. Both are worth investigating if full-time work is not available. Employees should take care to job-share with a compatible colleague. The most successful job-sharing arrangements seem to occur when two people agree duties and salary, and then persuade the employer to adopt the scheme.

Flexitime began more than twenty years ago, reportedly in Germany, when a group of workers staggered their arrival time in order to get to work across a busy street. Many employees find flexitime helps with commuting and family needs. For relocatees, unable to adopt conventional work schedules, flexitime may be a useful alternative. Another variation to consider is a *compressed working week*. This involves, depending on the occupation, stretching the working day – perhaps ten hours at work instead of eight – in order to allow the employee more time away from the workplace for recreation, study, family life.

A few more ideas for workers and volunteers

Find out what activities exist in your host environment. Some of the following may be available:

- international or local volunteer groups
- local colleges or open learning schemes
- informal international networks
- programmes initiated by other spouses
- corporate, government, community projects
- opportunities within the expatriate community
- openings for a 'home-country' flavoured service
- opportunities to write for local newspapers, in-house magazines
- 'foreign correspondent' type assignments for the home market.

8. Further Aspects of Employment on the Move

With this book, you have progressed through the main stages of exploring, searching and settling into employment on the move. There remain, however, a number of aspects of portable careers which you may want to know more about. For example:

- Is there any point in applying for a job now I am over 50?
- What do I do about age on my CV?
- How can organisations help working partners?
- I've never heard of Spouse Assistance Programmes – what are they?
- Is career counselling worthwhile?
- What about me – a trailing husband?
- How do I get a job when we go home?

There are no easy answers to these questions but the following may give you some ideas to think about and tips about finding out more for yourself.

Is there any point in applying for a job now I am over 50?

Every older person of whom I have asked this question replied with a resounding 'Yes'. Many declared their most exciting and satisfying careers began after 50 years of age and I know, from my own experience, they mean what they say. Now life expectancy for both men and women in Britain exceeds the Biblical 'three-score-years-and-ten', most of us can expect to live well into our mid-70s and beyond, and will be for the most part in good physical and mental shape. Thus, from the day we celebrate our half-century, we have several productive decades of life – more than infancy, childhood and adolescence put together – to look forward to and plan for.

Experts into ageing suggest physical exercise, healthy diet and a sensible lifestyle will help to maintain our energy and well-being. But, more recently, research has indicated how much more important is mental flexibility, a positive outlook and having a forward-looking enthusiasm for life. Many feel that work – paid or voluntary – is an essential element in an active long life.

It is worth remembering the idea of 'retirement' is a recent concept: in 1881, 73 per cent of Englishmen aged 65 and over were still employed; in 1981, the figure was only 11 per cent. Consider the following people who cease paid work *early*:

35 years: Boxers, dancers, wrestlers, rugby/soccer/tennis players
40 years: Divers, motor racing drivers, cricketers
45 years: Flat racing jockeys
50 years: Territorial Army members, off-shore riggers
55 years: Airline pilots, singers

Is there anything special about them? Yes, all their 'jobs' depend on physical stamina – and, most of them develop second, third and fourth 'careers' after their main job ceases. Of course, some people may *never* retire, such as actors, doctors, vicars, politicians, sovereigns and heads of state. As a generalisation, we could say their longevity depends on mental stamina, experience, maturity and wisdom – just the same attributes as most older workers say they possess.

So, if you are wondering if it is really worth all the effort of searching for a job once you reach 50 or whether to bother with employment again after early retirement, reconsider your options. The future may be longer than you think and it is important to have a meaningful structure to your life. As an individual you will benefit from involvement with other people, younger minds, a purpose in life and mental stimulation. Aim for the best and create a new career/life plan for the future. You may have retired from work or been made redundant by workplace or family changes, but you have not – and should not – retire from life.

What to do about age on your CV

Remind yourself: the objective of a CV or résumé is to gain an interview; it is not a full life history. When you send out your CV, you are trying to 'solve' an employer's problem by indicating how well your skills and experience match his needs. By offering personal data at too early a stage, you may only add to the employer's problem (and yours).

Some countries have strict laws governing the questions employers may ask. Age as a recruitment criterion seems to be a British speciality for, in the United States, France and Canada, age limits cannot be advertised and other countries, where legislation and official committees work against employment discrimination of *all* kinds, include Australia, Finland, Sweden and Germany.

Over-40s, women, minority groups, trailing spouses, the disabled, all find paid employment difficult because of ill-informed stereotypical images and prejudice. The earliest hurdle is at application stage. Functional or mixed CVs, résumés and 'biogs' are the simplest formats to use, as *you* choose the material you wish to include. The most difficult are personal dossiers and job application forms; these are full of awkward questions which are particularly hard to fill in and look untidy and suspicious with gaps and omissions.

Here are some tips and suggestions for overcoming awkward questions in written self-marketing communications and enhancing your chances of gaining a selection interview, but the results are not guaranteed!

- Use an up-to-date CV format or style.
- Omit or leave blank anything you feel may disadvantage you.
- Attach a (flattering) photograph.
- Write 'Not Applicable', 'Over 21' or similar instead of age details.
- Write 'see accompanying letter' and include your details there.

- Never describe yourself as a 'housewife' or 'out of work'.
- Omit any references to children, dependants, pets.
- Omit dates from school/further education examinations and detailed course contents.
- Avoid jobs requiring manual dexterity or physical strength if over 40. Instead, concentrate on service-type industries.
- Place your most recent or relevant experience immediately after your personal details, followed by your remaining work history in reverse order.
- Include educational information, without dates, towards the end.
- Emphasise your assets: your ability to work with others, maturity, good customer contacts, loyalty, reliability, sense of responsibility. Say how well you delegate, cope with change, manage others, make good decisions, keep cool.
- Concentrate the reader's attention on your excellent points: good literacy skills, balanced loyalties, open-mindedness, tolerance, cross-cultural experience, adaptability, self-discipline, good education.
- Do not undervalue yourself. An applicant who applies for a job in a lower than expected salary range may be suspected of being either desperate or useless.
- Indicate a motivated, positive attitude to the job. Show an interest in current affairs, business matters, education, environment, economics, computers.
- Imply good physical and mental health and fitness: mention bridge, crosswords, chess; active participation in teams, golf and other sports; committee work, voluntary posts of responsibility, research projects, Rotary and similar memberships.
- Mention advanced driving licence, computer familiarity, proficient languages and special skills. Include course details if presently studying and indicate expected achievements – for example, 'Degree expected Summer, 1993'.
- Always aim to be informed and informative, up-to-date and positive.

What can organisations do for working partners?

The simplest, cheapest and most positive step organisations can take to assist relocation success is to forget all about the old-fashioned, dependent 'trailing spouse'. Instead, expect your employee to have a 'Working Partner'. Surveys by the CBI, the Institute of Manpower Studies and many others continue to indicate that employees' concerns about spouse employment causes growing resistance to relocation. When transfers fail, the cost to employers is high; thousands of pounds, falling employee performance, squandered investment and departed key personnel. In comparison, corporate initiatives to assist working partners are very inexpensive indeed.

Both employee and partner want to be involved with the move from the start. They dislike imposed relocation and those where only very short notice is given prior to transfer. Include them at relocation planning stage to allow them to make personal decisions for themselves and their families, based on reliable facts rather than rumours, guesswork and 'knee-jerk' reactions.

Working partners want a smooth transition into employment in the new location as part of their own career continuity and development. Many working women are highly qualified professionals who simply cannot abandon patients, clients or customers in order to trail after their husbands at a moment's notice. For them as well as other dual-career couples, spouse employment assistance, a package to help find employment in the new location, is vital. Ideally, this should contain a range of services (there are more details in the next section which discusses spouse assistance programmes) from which individual partners choose elements appropriate to their personal needs.

But, it does not matter what variety, shape or form of spouse assistance is available, unless spouses are informed about it, it is useless. Communicate directly with employees' partners. Second-hand information, addressed to or carried home by the employee, is greatly resented and often disappears in transit. Letters, questionnaires, invitations and circulars must be addressed personally to spouses and sent *directly* to them.

Open access to a relocation information centre is welcomed.

This should contain local information about the host location – work permits, employment restrictions, directories, employment agencies, education and training facilities, etc – in order for spouses to research their own job opportunities. Photocopying, typewriting, free telephone and postal facilities are also much appreciated. Organisations can help with partners' retraining and examination fees, language and driving lessons, professional membership and conference subscriptions.

Relocating women welcome spouses' workshops or seminars organised by the company or their relocation consultants, if they are timed and located sensibly. Do not expect them to be enthusiastic about getting to a City Centre venue a moment or two after the school gates open on a Monday morning, please. These group sessions often create a core of friendship and support not only during the move but also afterwards. A 'family day' is another popular event: this enables all the relocating family or families to visit the new location where amusements may be provided for the children while their parents view promotional videos, listen to local speakers and discuss their individual situation with personnel. For pre-departure 'look-see' visits, working mothers may be grateful for the offer of child care; after the move, many single transferees need reliable practical help (plumbers, electricians). Another area where support is required, but neglected, is the care of older relatives: many middle-stage families take responsibility for ageing parents and other family members. Assistance with 'elder care', as the Americans call it, is a growing concern, unlikely to disappear in the foreseeable future.

When organisations adopt these measures and communicate them well, working partners begin to feel the company cares about their welfare and the relocation is more likely to succeed. The changed role of women from 'trailing spouse' to 'working partner' is here to stay, and those companies who adapt their attitude and actions to her will retain the competitive edge on those who do not.

Organisations can also assist spouses' employment by linking up with other firms, paying for career counselling services for spouses at off-site locations, supporting expatriate information resource initiatives, and – most importantly – offering their relocating personnel a family orientated training.

I've never heard of spouse assistance programmes – what are they?

Spouse assistance programmes aim to help the spouse of an employee find satisfactory employment in the new location. It may be a complete, fixed programme or a flexible package from which you choose elements, menu-style, most relevant to your situation. Usually it includes some or all of the following: career counselling, life planning, job search strategies, help with CVs and job applications. Sometimes employment opportunities, contacts and networking, a personal counselling element and follow-up support are included. The most important ingredient should be skills analysis, where transferable skills from all areas of life – home and community as well as paid employment – are thoroughly reviewed and linked into an action plan for your personal future.

As a working spouse, you can take the initiative in discovering if spouse assistance is available from both your partner's company *and* your own employer. Spouse assistance may have another name, or be unavailable until requested. Start with a general, open-ended question to personnel or the relocation manager, along the lines of 'What assistance can you offer me to find work in the new location?' If the answer is 'Nothing', suggest individual spouse assistance or career counselling yourself. Do not give up at the first refusal. Forward thinking organisations will encourage your interest and should pay all the costs. Spouse assistance may be provided by in-house personnel, relocation consultants or an outside specialist. Use the suggestions in the following section, Career Counselling, to check out the provider's suitability.

Other forms of help may come under the guise of spouse workshops or seminars, free office facilities, access to information centres, look-see and family visits. Take advantage of these to ensure that the company feels the effort has been worthwhile. You may be told the company will pay for a course, such as a TEFL course, which is fine provided it suits your personal needs. If it does not, suggest alternatives. Never simply refuse an offer – have your own suggestions ready as well. Ask if they can link with other companies in the host location for job opportunities or have access to data banks about education, training, employment agencies. Will they consider you as a freelance, teleworker, consultant, job-sharer, short-term contractor? Do they know the names of newspapers, journals, magazines in the new location? What about work permits and restrictions, overseas orientation programmes, briefings, induction seminars? And contacts and networks in embassies, consultants, town hall, chambers of commerce?

If you find it hard to obtain direct information from the company, it may be because the company believes that the limits of their responsibility are physical and financial aspects of the move. Anything more, in their eyes, could be seen as an intrusion into their employees' private lives. It may take longer to change corporate attitudes than the time available for your relocation, so tackle your partner for information about the move and spouse matters, read those in-house journals, look at the relocation literature, go to the presentations, join a partners' group. There may be more opportunities than you think.

Currently, many British companies remain wary of spouse assistance, perhaps fearing a deluge of unemployed women at their gates demanding instant answers to all their personal problems and career decisions. It is certainly unreasonable of you, the relocating working partner, to expect an organisation to become a guru on world-wide job vacancies or a corporate nanny for every aspect of the move. What is even more unreasonable, though, is for you to expect them to read your mind. Do not stay silent, passive and invisible when relocation occurs; ask for spouse assistance and use it. Not only will you help yourself, but you will also make it easier for those who follow after you.

Is career counselling worthwhile?

Still in a fog about the future and wondering about paying for career advice? Perhaps you remain uncertain after the exercises earlier in this book and feel it would be helpful to discuss your portable career with an expert who understands the whole business of testing, assessment and guidance. Whether you're redundant, retiring, relocating, returning or resettling, advertisements often suggest you can buy all the answers from around as little as £20 up to many thousands of pounds. Maybe a friend has recommended a particular vocational counsellor, and now she's the neighbourhood success story – you know, one of those who reads Marx while her husband cooks gourmet dinners and all her six children grow up trauma-free and go to Oxbridge!

But you hesitate: what will it cost, will it be worth it, need you pay for career help at all?

Career advice generally has a mixed reputation, especially among women. Many of us became disenchanted early on at school with those boring 'career' evenings. My first career, as a pianist, happened by default. As I loathed lacrosse and hockey, I spent hours playing the school piano and it was assumed I had real talent – an undiscovered musical prodigy, no less! My class teacher told my mother not to bother about a 'career' for me as I was not expected to pass any exams. Later, the truth emerged: yes, I liked music, but I was no genius. It took 20 more years for me to discover my academic potential, return to learning and make up for the lost time.

Vocational education has improved a great deal since then, but there remains a long way to go. 'Careers' remain a lower priority in many schools than university entrance statistics, while non-academic school-leavers may still receive only minimum help. Too often, youngsters are given only employment vacancy information and job descriptions and expected to get on with work, rather than the tools for planning and developing their careers.

What should you look for in a career counsellor?
American writer, Richard Bolles, suggests 'the three things you absolutely want from anyone you're paying good money to is a firm grasp of the whole job-hunting process, at its most creative and effective level; the ability to communicate information lucidly and clearly, (and) rapport with you.'

Guidelines for seeking professional career help

- Request a free, introductory, no-obligation talk before signing up.
- Ask exactly what the career counsellor will do. Explain your problem and find out how it is to be solved.
- Discover if the agency specialises in portable careers, has information about many kinds of work environment, is mainly for youngsters or redundant business people or is a corporate head-hunter. (There's nothing wrong with any of these, but I think you should know before signing up.)
- Find out who will be counselling you and their qualifications; how much one-to-one time you will have; the exact fees; if there is a comprehensive written and/or taped report and whether or not there is any follow-up support.
- Will you have to sit for hours taking batteries of tests? Is the tester qualified (The British Psychological Society maintains a members' Register of Competence in Occupational Testing)? How much importance is placed on such tests? What information will the tests provide? Is it appropriate for your situation? Is skills analysis provided – from all areas of life, paid and non-paid work?
- Take care with advisers who give vague, general advice; cannot communicate effectively; talk (in detail) about past clients or drop names; suggest a degree is the answer to everything (it isn't) or dismiss home, family, or non-paid experience.
- Go for the counsellor who expects you both to work together; helps to expand your horizons; possesses up-to-date, relevant information; acknowledges experience from both play groups and the boardroom and, *most importantly*, guides and supports you to help yourself.

Free career advice may be available at your local Careers Office (look it up in the BT or Thomson directory). Many careers offices advise only young school leavers but a few offer services to adults. Avoid busy times at Easter and the end of the summer term and ask for an appointment by telephone first. Even if individual help is unavailable, the Careers Office information resources (leaflets, publications, computer based information) with its COIC

Bookshop should be open for you to use. Details about free Educational Guidance Services for Adults (EGSAs) can be found at local public libraries, Citizens' Advice Bureaux and in reference books such as *Second Chances*. An *Adult Guidance Directory* is available from The Institute of Careers Guidance.

Fee-paying career services advertise in Yellow Pages, books, newspapers and magazines. Qualified professionals include members of the British Psychological Society or the Institute of Careers Guidance. Private vocational guidance costs vary and it is impossible to give fixed guidelines here apart from suggesting you compare several brochures and fee scales. You should expect to complete a detailed personal questionnaire, take pencil-and-paper tests, have face-to-face interview(s) and receive a written report. Some career advisers will spend several hours with an individual client, following the tests with visits spread over a day, a week or longer. Agencies offering telephone and postal help are best for specific information about a particular course or career rather than comprehensive advice and guidance. But, if you live far from other sources of help, or are homebound, perhaps this is worth a try. Do check through all the tips above first, though!

Is it really worth paying for career help at all? I believe it is, not just because it is the main focus of my work, but because my own life was given a jolt by career guidance – almost by accident. When my elder daughter was unsure about her A level choices but reluctant to have professional vocational help, I persuaded her towards it by agreeing to go too. On reading my report I was thoroughly astounded. 'You have an "uneducated" brain' wrote the consultant psychologist. He went on: 'I must emphasise that you undoubtedly have the necessary aptitudes to cope with further and higher studies . . .' And, I did.

For me, career guidance changed my life. Will it do the same for you? What if it does not work so well? There are no guarantees, but if the help, guidance and information which you receive is professional, unbiased, creative and *you*-orientated, you will have a clearer knowledge of your strengths and resources, increased opportunity to develop a portable career and more understanding of your occupational and personal development.

What about me – a trailing husband?

Up to now, research has paid little attention to the trailing male spouse, but as more women progress up the career ladder, a transferring male partner is expected to become increasingly apparent. The first noticeable difference between the sexes in response to mobility is that businesswomen usually consult their partners *before* the relocation decision is agreed. This should not be mistaken for asking a partner's 'permission' to relocate; it means working women discuss transfer arrangements at an earlier stage and more comprehensively than their male counterparts.

Because the traditional pattern is for men to place their careers before family or domestic concerns, those who do not conform to that way of life may experience problems. Organisational attitudes to the trailing husband, as described by Suzan Lewis and Cary Copper, suggest that it is more 'socially acceptable for the wife to follow her husband than vice versa'. Later, the accompanying male spouse may have restricted promotional opportunities and be perceived as lacking serious professional commitment. Fragmented or 'patchwork' CVs create difficulties for women, but men with 'stop-start' careers are regarded with even greater suspicion.

On a practical level, you, the relocating husband, should avoid unrealistic ideas about the time and effort needed to gain employment if this is the first time you have had to find work in and adjust to a strange location. Do not expect to find a job waiting for you upon arrival. If you have previously contacted expatriate or domestic employment agencies for assistance, keep in regular touch with them as they are unlikely to do all the work for you. All transferring partners – male or female – should take it upon themselves to know their transferable skills (with guidance when necessary), approach contacts and networks and start their own job search before leaving home.

If you are not already in an occupation or organisation where transfers are possible, you may be able to arrange a sabbatical or unpaid leave with your present employers and still have a job to come back to later. During your time away, your options include undergraduate, postgraduate and specialist training courses; a chance to try your hand at something new – perhaps that novel you have always thought about writing – or offer your expertise in the volunteer sector for little or no pay.

If your relocation is long term and there is little or no possibility of returning to your present home base, you should follow the job search advice in Chapter 3 and consider the portable careers suggestions earlier in this book, most of which are just as suitable to the trailing male as an accompanying wife.

How do I get a job when we go back home?

Returning home requires as much attention and preparation as any relocation. As far as your employment is concerned, if your portable career has been well planned to fit into a more comprehensive career/life pathway, then you should have an idea of your next step, or, at the very least, a sense of the best direction for your future. If not, return to Chapter 2, Information About Yourself, to re-evaluate your current situation.

You may have to start the job search all over again, particularly if you have been away for several years and find that the workplace has not stood still. Research the current work scene at home carefully before your posting is complete. Using ideas from Chapter 3, read the British press (if abroad) or your hometown newspaper, pay special attention to current job advertisements, to familiarise yourself with expanding or contracting fields of work and present day salaries. Consider a refresher or updating course to brush up your skills, give you confidence, new contacts, an extra dimension to your CV and current references. You feel more effective and professional if you have interviews pre-arranged, but you must still illustrate how mobility has kept you up-to-date and in touch.

Refresh contacts with your former colleagues for news and opportunities with your former employer. Use home visits for informal get-togethers and offer your services – without pay if necessary – as a 'foreign' correspondent, researcher, consultant, field officer. Renew subscriptions to professional journals, network newsletters, in-house magazines. Keep your name in front of former employers. Attend conferences, workshops or seminars linked to your former or preferred field of work and introduce yourself to other delegates.

A final word here about the personal aspects of returning home after a long period abroad: the 're-entry' process is much underestimated and could be much more traumatic than you imagine. People and places will have changed, lifestyle is different but your memories of 'home' will have stayed the same or even become rose-tinted. It is wise to assume you will experience a degree of culture shock when you return home after a period abroad and will require time to adjust. Take note of suggestions for settling in, in Chapter 6, and allow yourself time to adjust gradually to life back home.

Who knows, maybe soon there will be another 'irresistible offer', to echo Joanna Foster (see Afterword, page 141), another relocation to Peru, Pakistan, Poland or Pennsylvania. Or, perhaps you will be settling somewhere in Britain – away from a garrison, industrial estate, or commuter belt. Once you have arrived, unpacked your bags and found the teapot, your portable career can be taken out again, dusted down and put to work.

Bon Voyage and Good Luck!

Afterword: Mobility and Equal Opportunities

by Joanna Foster, Chair of the Equal Opportunities Commission

(The following is part of a speech given to the CBI Employee Relocation Council's annual conference in May 1988. In October 1991, Joanna Foster wrote this to me: 'If I was to speak on the subject today, I would link very forcibly the current concern to be family friendly with relocation packages, counselling and the European Market'. My asterisks indicate changes since 1988.)

I believe mobility is one of the key equal opportunity work/ family issues about which we should be concerned and, as Chair of the EOC, I am very keen to discuss the issues and to help with solving what is increasingly an economic business problem as well as a personal one. The cost on our businesses and the cost on our families is too high to continue disregarding the human side of relocation . . . .

. . . I would like to bring in my own personal experience to highlight what I believe are some of the main issues. I have been what the US relocation jargon calls a trailing spouse – ie those of us who are relocated because of our other half's career move. I am also half of a dual career couple.

We got married *27 years ago, a '60s' couple living in swinging, revolting, bra-burning, liberated Britain. Employment was high, wages were high, the EEC was in its infancy, managers moved without questioning their company's wisdom and wives and families did the same. Women were only 40 per cent of the workforce and a small percentage of managers were women. It was rare to find a female business school graduate, line manager or accountant.

Marriage meant you probably had an interesting job which brought in 'pin' money, and children meant you 'settled down' and were home based for probably 15 years. At school girls were steered almost exclusively into the caring and support professions and needlework and domestic science were the foundations for a lifetime of bliss. Doing a shorthand and typing course opened every door and knights on white chargers were the breadwinners. Tarzan reigned supreme and Jane, of course, was the silent power behind the throne.

We, as a couple, were neither liberated, revolting or unconventional. I started my working life as a secretary and although I never 'settled down' I have had a fairly typical 'stop–start', 'patchwork' career, with stops for children and stops because of relocation. Our life now, though not typical, does underline some of the mobility/equal opportunities issues.

We now live in Oxford. Our two children are *teenagers. Five days a week, my husband commutes to London. I join him on the train for one. For two others I travel to Manchester and stay overnight and the fifth day I might be travelling to Aberdeen, Aberystwyth, Bournemouth, Bootle or Brussels. Twice a month, my husband travels to **Milan to his head office.

We don't live in London or Manchester or between the two because we have spent 10 years of our lives moving country and now with *GCSEs pending and elderly parents getting more and more dependent, our house finally being as we want it, staying put makes sense.

It is though, the thoughts about our 10 mobile years, that I want to share and although our moves were international, I believe the experience is comparable to moving around the UK. The cultural difference can well be greater in one's own country. Seeing the world regularly now from a Manchester perspective it looks different to Oxford and London. Yesterday I was in Edinburgh and it became very clear to me there as well!

We started moving when the children were babies – highly portable literally. My husband had been offered an irresistible job at INSEAD, the international business school in Fontainebleau and it seemed a good moment to put my career as a management trainer with the Industrial Society on hold. Little did I know then it would be on hold for 10 years and little did I realise then what an effect moving around was to have on both our careers and our family life.

In France I worked with the wives of the MBA students and the wives of the middle and senior managers who were sent to the business school to learn about international trade. Their wives and families were also learning the lessons of high mobility. From Paris to Pittsburgh, Pennsylvania – the number two corporate city in the USA, experiencing colossal changes with the run down of old industries – steel – birth of new technologies/sunrise industry. It was a move I did not welcome and which initially I found very hard. No work visa. No friends or family and as someone once said, separated by a common language. I was culture shocked and it took six months to really find my feet and adjust and that had, needless to say, a knock-on effect on my family. It was, however, my own culture shock and the stress that goes with it that got me moving and got me involved in work which professionally led me to what I now do. Based at the University of Pittsburgh – at their nationally respected Western Psychiatric Institute and Clinic – I was involved with Pittsburgh companies, helping them develop relocation packages and stress management programmes which focused on the effects of mobility in organisations, managers and their families and the effects on women's career development.

Three years later we were back in the UK, based in Oxford – kids into local schools and British educational system for the first time – my husband had a local job at the Oxford Management Centre – now Templeton College – and me by now anxious to embark seriously on what for the first time I regarded as my career. Three years later my husband was lured back – another 'irresistible offer' – to INSEAD for three years. He commuted weekly from Oxford to Paris. *Six months ago his work base changed to London.

For three years whilst setting up the equal opportunities unit, The Pepperell Unit at The Industrial Society, I have increasingly learned that relocation epitomises one of the extremely difficult dilemmas facing organisations, managers and their families.

Companies which are increasingly practising equal opportunities, are realising it is no longer wise to assume people, men or women will or will not move – as Leeds Permanent Building Society learned after they assumed their men were mobile and their women were not. (The EOC formally investigated their mobility policies.)

It is prudent to invest time and energy putting money into looking at how one can best help managers and their families.

We need to find ways of mitigating the stress and disruptive effects of relocation. And I would add that we need above all to recognise – and *publicly* recognise – the relocation/family dilemma in our personnel, employee relations, equal opportunity and relocation programmes and packages.

* *in 1988*
** *now at the London Business School*

References

Adler, Nancy J (1991) *International Dimensions of Organizational Behaviour*, 2nd Edn. PWS-KENT Publishing Company, Boston USA

Adler, Nancy J and Izraeli, Dafna N (1988) *Women in Management Worldwide*, M.E. Sharpe Inc, New York & London

Alston, Anna (1987) *Equal Opportunities*, Penguin

Altman, Forster, Greenbury and Munton (in press) *Managing Relocation*, John Wiley & Sons Ltd

Barber, Thelma (1986) *Careers and Jobs without O-Levels*, Hobsons

Bastress, Frances (1986) *The Relocating Spouse's Guide to Employment*, Woodley Publications, USA

Bolles, Richard (1986 and 1991) *What Color Is Your Parachute?* Ten Speed Press

Brockman, T (1990) *The Job Hunter's Guide to Japan*, Kodansha International, Tokyo & New York

Coyle, Wendy (1988) *On The Move*, Hampden Press, Sydney, NSW, Australia

Crites John (1981) *Career Counselling*, McGraw-Hill

Ekstrom, Ruth B *Project HAVE Skills*, Educational Testing Services, New Jersey USA

Figler, Howard, PhD (1988) *The Complete Job-Search Handbook*, Henry Holt and Company, New York USA

Greenbury, Linda (1988) 'Relocating the Working Wife', *Relocation News* No 5

Greenbury, Linda (1990) 'Relocating single women abroad and at home', *Relocation News* No 13

Greenbury, Linda (1992) 'Just a Husband, the trailing male spouse', *Relocation News* No 21

Greenbury, Linda (1991) Assistance for the Working Spouse, Relocation Factsheet, Black Horse Relocation

Griffiths, Susan (1991) *Teaching English Abroad*, Vacation Work, Oxford

Hopson, Barry and Scally, Mike (1984) *Build Your Own Rainbow*, Mercury

Jones, Roger (1991) *How to Live and Work in Australia*, How to Books

Josefowitz, Natasha and Gadon, Herman (1988) *Fitting In*, Addison Wesley

Lewis, Suzan and Cooper Cary L (1989) *Career Couples*, Unwin Paperbacks

Mills, Steve (1988) *How to Live and Work in America*, How to Books

Onslow, Barbara (1983) *What Can A Teacher Do Except Teach?* MSC (COIC)

Raban, A J (1991) *Working in the European Community*, Office for Official Publications of the European Community, Hobsons Publishing PLC

Rossman, Marlene L (1986) *The International Businesswoman*, Praeger, New York & London

Shortland, Sue (1990) *Relocation: A Practical Guide*, IPM

Veltman, Laura (1990) *How to Live and Work in Australia*, 2nd Edn. How to Books

Useful Resources

Books

Titles published by Kogan Page

An A–Z of Careers and Jobs, 5th Edn, Diane Burston

British Qualifications (annual)

Directory of Higher Education Institutions in the European Community

Going Freelance, 3rd Edn, Godfrey Golzen

The Good Retirement Guide, (annual), Rosemary Brown

Great Answers to Tough Interview Questions, 3rd Edn, Martin John Yate

A Guide to Higher Education Systems and Qualifications in the European Community

Higher Education in the European Community: The Student Handbook

How to Master Selection Tests, Mike Bryon and Sanjay Modha

How to Study, Anne Howe

The Job Assault Course, M C Lindsay Stewart (for armed service personnel)

Job Sharing: A Practical Guide, Pam Walton

The Kogan Page Mature Student's Handbook, 3rd Edn, Margaret Korving

Manage Your Own Career: A Self-Help Guide to Career Choice and Change, Ben Ball

The Mid Career Action Guide, 2nd Edn, Derek Kemp and Fred Kemp

Moving Up, Stan Crabtree

101 Ways to Succeed as an Independent Consultant, Timothy R V Foster

Talk Small, Pete Daly
Test Your Own Aptitude, 2nd Edn, Jim Barrett and Geoff Williams
Working Abroad: The Daily Telegraph Guide to Living and Working Overseas, (annual), Godfrey Golzen
Working for Yourself, (annual) Godfrey Golzen
Working for Yourself in the Arts and Crafts, 2nd Edn, Sarah Hosking

The Kogan Page careers series, although written mainly for school and college leavers, contains practical and inexpensive books on a wide variety of professions and careers including: *Careers in Alternative Medicine, Careers in Environmental Conservation, Careers in Home Economics, Careers in Journalism, Careers in Nursing and Allied Professions, Careers in Photography, Careers in Sport, Careers in the Travel Business* and many more.

Other publications

Adult Guidance Directory, The Institute of Careers Guidance, 27a Lower High Street, Stourbridge, West Midlands DY8 1TA
An MBA Guide to Business Schools, Pitman Publishing in association with the Association of MBAs
Build Your Own Rainbow, Barrie Hopson and Mike Scally, Mercury
Careers Opportunities for Anyone, Anne Purbon, Hobsons
Economist's Guide to . . . (various countries)
EFL Careers Guide, from EFL Ltd, 64 Ormly Road, Ramsey, Isle of Man
Equal Opportunities – A Careers Guide, Anna Alston, Penguin
Handbook for Women Travellers, Maggie and Gemma Moss, Piatkus
How to Make Money from Freelance Writing, Andrew Crofts, Piatkus
How to Teach Abroad, Roger Jones, How To Books, Plymouth
International Guide to Qualifications in Education (academic), compiled by the British Council, Mansell Publishing Ltd
Internships 1992, Peterson's, New Jersey USA
KOMPASS, published in each country
Managing Stress, David Fontana, BPS/Routledge
Networking and Mentoring: A Woman's Guide, Dr Lily M. Segerman-Peck, (1991) Piatkus
Official Guide to MBA Programs, published by GMAT Program Direction Office, Educational Testing Service, PO Box 6106, Princeton, New Jersey 08541-6106 USA
Running your own Bed and Breakfast, Elizabeth Gundrey, Piatkus

Second Chances: National Guide to Adult Education and Training, (1992) 8th edn, Pates & Good (COIC)
Social Skills at Work, David Fontana, BPS/Routledge
Springboard Women's Development Workbook, Liz Willis and Jenny Daisley, Hawthorn Press
Teaching English Abroad, Susan Griffiths, Vacation Work, Oxford
Thinking about Volunteering, Returned Volunteer Action (RVA), 1 Amwell Street, London EC1R 1VL
UK Directory of Educational Guidance Services for Adults, UDACE, published by National Educational Guidance Initiative, c/o YHAFHE, Bowling Green Terrace, Leeds LS11 9SX
Volunteer Work, Central Bureau, Seymour Mews House, Seymour Mews, London W1H 9PE
What Color Is Your Parachute? Richard Bolles, Ten Speed Press
A Woman in your Own Right, Anne Dickson, Quartet
Writers' and Artists' Yearbook (annual) A and C Black
The Writer's Handbook (annual), Barry Turner, Macmillan

Useful Addresses

Arts Council of Great Britain, 14 Great Peter Street, London SW1P 3NQ
Association of British Travel Agents, Waterloo House, 11–17, Chertsey Road, Woking, Surrey GU12 5AL
Association of Commonwealth Universities, John Foster House, 36 Gordon Square, London WC1 0PF
British Association for Counselling, 1 Regent Place, Rugby, Warwickshire CV21 2PJ
British Council, Medlock Street, Manchester M15 4PR
British Dietetic Association, 7th Floor, Elizabeth House, 22 Suffolk Street, Queensway, Birmingham B1 1LS
British Institute of Professional Photography, Fox Talbot House, Amwell End, Ware, Herts SG12 9HN
British Library-Newspapers, Colindale Avenue, London NW9 5HE (071-323 7353)
British Psychological Society, St Andrew's House, 48 Princess Road East, Leicester LE1 7DR
British Red Cross, 9 Grosvenor Crescent, London SW1X 7EJ
British Society of Music Therapists, 69 Avondale Avenue, East Barnet, Hertfordshire EN4 8NB

British Veterinary Nursing Association, Seedbed Centre, Coldharbour Road, Harlow, Essex CM19 5AF

Business and Technology Education Council (BTEC), Upper Woburn Place, London WC1H 0HH

Business Information Network, 25 Southampton Buildings, London WC2A 1AX

Business Women's Travel Club, 520 Fulham Road, London SW6 5NJ

Central Bureau for Educational Visits and Exchanges, Seymour Mews House, Seymour Mews, London W1H 9PE

Centre for International Briefing, Farnham Castle, Farnham, Surrey GU9 0AG

Chartered Society of Designers, 29 Bedford Square, London WC1B 3ED

City Business Library, 106 Fenchurch Street, London EC3M 5JB

City & Guilds of London Institute, 76 Portland Place, London W1N 4AA

Clothing and Footwear Industry, 105 Butlers Wharf Business Centre, Curlew Street, London SE1 2ND

COIC, Room E414 Moorfoot, Sheffield S1 4PQ

Commonwealth Institute, Kensington High Street, London W8 6NG

Commonwealth Secretariat, Marlborough House, Pall Mall, London SW1Y 5HX

Confederation of British Industries (CBI) Employee Relocation Council, Centre Point, 103 New Oxford Street, London WC1A 1DU

Council for National Academic Awards (CNAA), 344–354 Gray's Inn Road, London WC1X 8BP

Council for the Accreditation of Correspondence Colleges, 27 Marylebone Road, London, NW1 5JS

Department of Trade & Industry, 1–19 Victoria Street, London SW1H 0ET

Department of Transport, 2 Marsham Street, London SW1P 3EB

ECCTIS 2000, Fulton House, Jessop Avenue, Cheltenham GL50 3SH

Employment Conditions Abroad, Anchor House, 15 Britten Street, London SW3 3TY

English Language Unit, The British Council, Medlock Street, Manchester M15 4PR

Equal Opportunities Commission, Overseas House, Quay Street, Manchester M3 3HN

European Women's Management Development Network: UK Representative – Christine Barham, 23 Station Road, Cheddington, Nr Leighton Buzzard, Bedfordshire LU7 0SG

FOCUS Information Services, St Mary Abbot's Hall, Vicarage Gate, London W8 4HN

Fulbright Commission, 6 Porter Street, London W1M 2HR

HMSO: Telephone orders 071-873 9090 General enquiries 071-873 0011

Hotel and Catering Training Company, International House, High Street, Ealing, London W5 5DB

Hotel Catering and Institutional Management Association, 191 Trinity Road, London SW17 7HN

Incorporated Society of Musicians, 10 Stratford Place, London W1N 9AE

Institute of Baths & Recreation Management, Gifford House, 36–38 Sherrard Street, Melton Mowbray, Leicestershire LE13 1XJ

Institute of Careers Guidance, 27a Lower High Street, Stourbridge, West Midlands DY8 1TA

Institute of Home Economics, Aldwych House, 71–91 Aldwych, London WC2B 4HN

Institute of Leisure and Amenity Management, Lower Basildon, Reading, Berkshire RG8 9NE

Institute of Linguists, 24a Highbury Grove, London N5 2EA

Institute of Personnel Management, 35 Camp Road, London SW19 4UX

Interior Decorators and Designers Association Ltd, 102–104 Church Road, Teddington, Middlesex TW11 8PY

International Health and Beauty Council, PO Box 36, Arundel, West Sussex BN18 0SW

International Society of Work Options c/o FOCUS, 509 Tenth Avenue East, Seattle, Washington 98102

Iyengar Yoga Institute, 223 Randolph Avenue, London W9 1NL

National Association for Voluntary Organisations, 26 Bedford Square, London WC1B 3HU

National Association of Volunteer Bureaux, St Peter's College, College Road, Saltley, Birmingham B8 3TE

National Coaching Foundation, 4 College Close, Becketts Park, Leeds LS3 3QH

National Council for Vocational Qualifications, 222 Euston Road, London NW1 2BZ

National Council for Voluntary Organisations, 26 Bedford Square, London WC1B 3HU

National Extension College, 18 Brooklands Avenue, Cambridge CB2 2HN

National Federation of Women's Institutes, 104 New King's Road, London SW6 4LY

National Institute of Adult Continuing Education, 19b de Montfort Street, Leicester LE1 7GE

National Women's Register, National Office, 9 Bank Plain, Norwich NR2 4SL

Open College, FREEPOST, Warrington WA2 7DR

Open College of the Arts, Houndhill, Worsbrough, Barnsley, South Yorkshire S70 6TU

Open University, Central Enquiries, PO Box 71, Walton Hall, Milton Keynes MK7 6AA

Overseas Development Administration, Abercrombie House, Eaglesham Road, East Kilbride, Glasgow G75 8EA

Oxfam, 274 Banbury Road, Oxford OX2 7DZ

Pepperell Unit, The Industrial Society, Robert Hyde House, 48 Bryanston Square, London W1H 7LN

Pre-School Playgroups Association, 61–63 King's Cross Road, London WC1X 9LL

Redwood Women's Training Association, (Sue Turner) 5 Spennithorne Road, Skellow, Doncaster, South Yorkshire DN6 8PF

Retired Executive Action Clearing House, 89 Southwark Street, London SE1 0HD

Returned Volunteer Action, 1 Amwell Street, London EC1R 1VL

Royal British Legion, 48 Pall Mall, London SW1Y 5JY

Royal Institute of British Architects, 66 Portland Place, London W1N 4AD (ask for the Overseas Division if relevant)

Save the Children Fund, 17 Grove Lane, London SE5 8RD

(Shiatsu) East/West Centre, 188 Old Street, London EC1V 9BP

Society of Teachers of Alexander Technique, 10 London House, 266 Fulham Road, London SW10 9EL

Success After Sixty, 40–41 Old Bond Street, London W1X 3AF

Soldiers', Sailors' and Airmen's Families Association/Forces Help Society (SSAFA/FHS), 16–18 Old Queen Street, London SW1H 9HP

Sports Council, 16 Upper Woburn Place, London WC1H 0QP

United Nations Information Centre, Ship House, 20 Buckingham Gate, London SW1E 6LB

University of London Centre for Extra-Mural Studies, 26 Russell Square, London WC1B 5DQ

University of the Third Age (U3A) c/o BASSAC, 13 Stockwell Road, London SW9 9AU

Voluntary Service Overseas (VSO), 317 Putney Bridge Road, London SW15 2PN

Wine and Spirit Education Trust, Five Kings House, 1 Queen Street Place, London EC4R 1QS

Women's Corona Society, 35 Belgrave Square, London SW1X 8QB

Women in Management, 64 Marryat Road, London SW19 5BN

Workers' Educational Association, 9 Upper Berkeley Street, London W1H 8BY

Working Mothers Association, 77 Holloway Road, London N7 8JZ

YMCA Overseas & National Office, 640 Forest Road, London E17 3DZ

YWCA Overseas Office, 16 Great Russell Street, London WC1B 3LR

Career counselling services

Career Counselling Services, 46 Ferry Road, London SW13 9PW

Career Development Centre for Women, 97 Mallard Place, Twickenham, Middlesex TW1 4SW

Career Relocations Ltd, 1st Floor, 11 Garrick Street, London WC2E 9AR

Careers for Women, 4th Floor, 2 Valentine Place, London SE1 8QH

Focus Career Services, 19 Kattenberg, 1170 Brussels, Belgium

WICE, Boulevard du Montparnasse 20, 75015 Paris, France